Red Ladies In Waiting

By Hans-Heiri Stapfer
Color By Tom Tullis

squadron/signal publications

A MiG-15bis and an An-2 Colt rest in the grass at the Aeroking storage depot at Vecses, Hungary. It is hoped that one day these aircraft might be restored and placed in a museum.

ISBN 0-89747-316-7

If you have any photographs of aircraft, armor, soldiers or ships of any nation, particularly wartime snapshots, why not share them with us and help make Squadron/Signal's books all the more interesting and complete in the future. Any photograph sent to us will be copied and the original returned. The donor will be fully credited for any photos used. Please send them to:

Squadron/Signal Publications, Inc.
1115 Crowley Drive.
Carrollton, TX 75011-5010

Acknowledgements:

Viktor Kulikov
George Punka
Peter Nagy
Robert Bock
Marcus Fulber
Martin Baumann
Hans-Georg Volprich
Anton Wettstein
Harald Ziewe
Wolfgang Tamme
A.A. Zirnov
Eckhardt Prell
Luftwaffen-Forum
Bundeswehr
S.A. Gorbachev
Viktor K. Kabanov
Otakar Saffek
Yefim Gordon

Igor Shejin
Andras Nagy
Aeroking K. F. T.
Wojoiech Luczak
Jens Schymura
Hans-Joachim Mau
Deutsche Lufthansa
Matthias Grunder
Andreas Schutz
Hans Schreiber
Sukhoi OKB
V. Hoeveler
Soldat & Technik
Martin Baumann
MiG OKB
ZLINEK Magazine
Josef Simon
Nick Waters

All photographs were taken by the author unless otherwise credited.

Dedication:

This book is dedicated to Budapest, the most impressive city I have ever visited. It is not the mighty buildings alone, but rather the friendly and warm hearted habitants that make this jewel on the Danube river into the place that I always return to with pleasure. I wish that my home town, Zurich, had half of the charming life style of Budapest. The fact is that the inhabitants of Zurich show a joy of life equal to that of the average visitor to a cemetery. The famous Palinka brandy and excellent Hungarian wines combine to make Budapest a little bit heaven on earth.

Overleaf: Former-Hungarian Air Force MiG-15 Fagots and MiG-17 Frescos await their final fate on a large dump near Budapest. This was rather typical for most Warsaw Pact countries of the period, where a great many aircraft were moved to storage depots where they were stripped of usable material, then scrapped.

Squadron Signal's most handsome (and to date the only) Swiss author, Hans-Heiri Stapfer poses in front of a MiG-23 Flogger at Moscow's Khodinka Airfield during the Summer of 1992. He was wearing a T-shirt with the insignia of the 44th Bomb Group, 8th Air Force, a gift from a Second World War Liberator pilot from the 44th.

Author's Note

This book is a result of my various trips into the former Eastern Bloc countries. It is a pictorial retrospective of the early 1990s, when Communism ceased to exist east of the Iron Curtain. This period saw a great deal of change in military aviation within the former Warsaw Pact nations.

While writing this book, a lot of fine memories came back to me. During my stay in the former Soviet Union, I resided with Viktor Kulikov and his wife Irina, her Russian cooking will be missed. Igor Shejin showed me how to survive the time between the first drink of Vodka and breakfast the next day. His advice was very much appreciated. To all of them I owe a sincere **Balshoj Spasiba!**

As always, I have best recollections of Budapest. The hospitality was, and still is, outstanding and I feel that many of us Westerners could learn from Eastern European hospitality. George Punka and his wife were always extremely helpful. Far beyond what I could expect, as was Andras Nagy and his family. A special thanks for the splendid dinners must go to the Eiler family, especially its very charming daughter. The trips to the Hungarian capital give me insight into the expanded night life since the fall of the Communist government, which was well beyond the limits of my financial budget, but the funny time in the **Oazis** Night club was well worth it. So again I say **Koszonom szepen** to all my friends in Hungary.

During my various trips into the former Warsaw Pact countries I quickly realized that **Perestroika** had not only its shining side. After more than forty years under Communism the people of Eastern Europe eagerly wanted the sweet taste of capitalism and endless shopping. Most of these people were not aware of the fact that the Golden West and the free enterprise system also had its shortcomings.

It happened that most of the tight social structures broke down in these countries and was replaced by Western oriented business behavior. One of the nice things I remembered was that the people during the Communist era had time — time for a small talk or time for a beer. It was the warmth of their nature that I always liked in Eastern Europe. More warmth and less cool business behavior would be something I would appreciate here in my own country, Switzerland

Last but not least, I would like to give my sincere thanks to all the friends and institutions who willingly supported me with the information and photographs that made this book possible. I would also like to take this opportunity to thank squadron/signal's editor, Nick Waters, for his efforts on this and all my previous books.

Introduction

When Mikhail Sergeyevich Gorbachev came to power as Secretary General of the Communist Party after the death of Chernevkov during early 1985, none of the politicians and observers on either side of the Iron Certain were aware that this man would radically change the Soviet Empire. The changes he put in place altered the structure of the Soviet Union more than any leader since the Bolsheviks came to power in 1917.

The catchwords, **Perestroika** (the restructuring of the Soviet economy and Communist Party) and **Glasnost** (openness) have now come to stand for total reform of the Communist system. This reform has led to a restructuring of most of the political systems in Europe.

The situation within the USSR that Gorbachev inherited was immensely depressing. The Soviet economy was in terrible shape, except for those areas involved in the production of defense material and space technology. In consumer goods, the Soviet Union resembled a Third World state rather than an industrial superpower.

This was the result of the Soviet policy that every Ruble should go into arms production in order to keep up with Western innovations in weapons technology. At the beginning of the Cold War, during the Stalin era, the East could keep up with the West; but as the arms race heated up, the cost of arms development and production slowly caused the subsequent economic collapse of the Soviet empire.

A line-up of Rumanian Air Force MiG-21F-13 Fishbed Cs. The Fishbed was numerically the most important aircraft of the Warsaw Pact. During the Cold War period, Rumania was the country.with the closest links to the West. Now, Rumania stands alone in Europe and is far behind the reform process. (Ion Lupescu)

Many former Warsaw Pact combat aircraft, especially earlier generation aircraft, are now resting in storage/salvage depots and are an unwanted heritage of the Communist era. These two early MiG-21F-13 Fishbed Cs, along with the nearby MiG-15 rear fuselage, once proudly flew with the Hungarian Air Force, before cutbacks in the force made them un-necessary. Similar storage/salvage dumps have been seen in other Eastern Bloc countries. In most cases, needed or useful parts are stripped from the aircraft, then they are held awaiting the final decision to scrap them.

Gorbachev's main fault was that he had believed that Perestroika and Glasnost could raise the standard of living within the Soviet Union and raise the level of the economy. In fact, after only five years *Perestroika* became the most important factor in the end of the then mighty Soviet Union.

When the Soviet Union ceased to exist on New Year's day 1992, the Soviets had seen the fall of Berlin Wall, the reunion of Germany and the retreat of Soviet troops from all the former Soviet satellites. The Commonwealth of Independent States (CIS), an organization intended to replace the former USSR, was put in place to represent the eleven different Republics that made up the former Soviet Union. These Republics are: Armenia, Azerbaijan, Byelorussia, Modavia, Kazakhstan, Kirghizia, Russia, Tajikistan, Turkmenia, Ukraine, and Uzbekistan. None of these Republics have, as yet, shown any intention of solving the economic and ethnic problems they inherited from the former Soviet Union.

In many ways the changes initiated by Gorbachev came too fast, for both the East and West. They did not allow for assistance to be generated by the West to help reshape the Soviet economy. The changes took the world by surprise and there was just no time to react before the collapse took place.

Most of the people in the Communist counties had a totally wrong idea of what life in the West under a free enterprise system was really like.

For many they thought the changes would lead to a life style like they had seen on the *"Dallas"* TV series. Many thought they would now have a lot money and be able to buy anything they needed. The reality proved to be much more frustrating.

The Communist society was notorious for its economic inefficiency. Unemployment was not known in these countries and the lack of consumer goods was balanced to a certain extent by this social safety net.

When the Russian President Boris Yeltsin announced the implementation of a free enterprise economic system and democracy, it was not the same as most Westerners understand. Basically the Communist structure remained in place. Former Apparatchik now called themselves Managers. Former members of the Polit Bureau and high ranking members of the Communist Party purchased the factories, buildings and, as a result, the same people are now running the economy.

The CIS must produce sufficient quantities of consumer goods in order to survive and prosper. The people; however, do not understand how a free enterprise system works and, as a result, this is a difficult and dangerous time for the former Soviet Union!

It is believed that there are about 20 million citizens of the former Soviet Union that want to emigrate to Western Europe and North America. The results of such a wave of emigrants would be catastrophic for Western economies which could not support such a population increase.

With the decline of the Soviet Union and its fixed prices for consumer goods, the prices of most goods have exploded. Within a year, for example, the cost for a loaf of bread went from 20 Kopecks to 30 Rubles, which is an inflation rate of more than 15,000 percent. Salaries, in turn, were raised slowly and could not hope to match the rising prices. By the Summer 1992, the average salary of a Russian worker was the equivalent of twenty U.S. dollars per month.

With this inflation rate, it is hardly surprising that the average citizen of the former Soviet Union would prefer hard currency (such as dollars)

Half a decade ago, no one could have possibly guessed that former East German MiG-29 Fulcrum air superiority fighters would be wearing the Iron Cross and Black/Red/Yellow fin flash national insignia of West Germany. The MiG-29 Fulcrum was one of the few combat types that were absorbed into the West German forces as a result of the reunification of the two German republics. Most former East German aircraft were either sold or scrapped. (Klaus Meissner)

over the Ruble for his efforts. According to some estimates, there are approximately eight million U.S. dollars stored by individuals within the former Soviet Union. Other estimates state that up to a third of all dollar bills issued by the United States government are now within the territory of the former Soviet Union. This has led to the formation of a Russian Mafia. In May of 1990, the Mafia ceased to be a source of entertainment and the organization had spread into inter-regional groups with international connections. Ethnic group specialization is common. The Chechen Mafia specializes in Gold, a Jewish Mafia in computers, and the Moldavians in stolen cars. The demand for hard currency within the CIS has led to a healthy Black Market, even in weapons.

When the Soviet Union devolved, it had some 6, 611 combat aircraft and some 1,838 attack helicopters in its inventory. In order to meet international treaty obligations, the CIS had reduced these numbers to 5,150 combat aircraft and 1,500 attack helicopters.

The latest figures from the defense industry indicates that up to two million workers could be laid off unless some way is found to convert these facilities from defense related production to consumer goods production. It is estimated that total production in the CIS was some thirty percent lower during 1992 than the previous year and it is believed that up to fifty percent of the population is unemployed. Most of the former Warsaw Pact countries are in this same situation. Even the former East Germany, which has had the benefit of a large investment from West Germany, still has massive unemployment. This was not the expectation of the East Germans, who thought that, after the reunification on 3 October 1990, the economy would improve. In fact, most key economic and government positions in the former East Germany were quietly and

quickly taken over by West Germans. Many companies and factories were either liquidated by West Germany or came under control of West German corporations.

One of the main problems of the former Eastern Bloc nations is that their products, apart from a few goods, are of such inferior quality, that they cannot be sold with success on Western markets. Consumers in most countries have favored Western produced products over those produced in the Eastern Bloc and this has had devastating results for the CIS economy.

This all has led to a surplus of aircraft and no budgets for maintaining and operating the aircraft that remain in the inventory. In most former Warsaw Pact nations, the surplus aircraft will be scrapped. Germany has announced that it will sell or scrap all combat aircraft that it obtained from the former East Germany with the exception of the MiG-29s. Other countries are also storing or scraping their excess combat aircraft. The supply of spare parts for those aircraft still operational is a serious problem and drastically impacts on combat readiness in most former Warsaw Pact nations. As a result, many are seeking partnerships with Western companies to upgrade existing aircraft with Western equipment. One such example is Rumania and Israel who have entered into an agreement to upgrade the MiG-21 with Western electronics and other equipment that will allow the aircraft to remain in service for the fore-seeable future. Other nations would like to replace their Russian equipment with U.S. equipment, but a shortage of hard currency hampers these plans.

In the meantime, many of the former bases of the Soviet Air Force are now storage sites for a wide variety of military aircraft, making these locations the home for large numbers of Red Ladies in Waiting.

5

A British-built Sopwith 1 1/2 Strutter of the Imperial Air Force Flying School, which was located at Khodinka during the Spring of 1917. The roundels applied on the tail and undersurfaces were the markings of the Russian Imperial Army. (Viktor Kulikov)

A Royal Air Force Be-2c with ski-undercarriage at the Flying School during the Winter of 1917. A group of RAF instructors, under the command of British Major J. Valentine, trained Russian pilots and ground crewmen on various British-built aircraft. The aircraft were subsequently handed over to the Imperial Russian Air Force and received full Russian markings. (Viktor Kulikov)

Khodinka Airfield

Khodinka, also known as Frunze, Airfield, is located on the Leningradshij Prospect (Leningrad Avenue) in the center of Moscow and is considered by many to be the birthplace of Russian aviation. The field is located near the famous Dynamo Station and the Aeroport underground stations. Khodinka Airfield, the former Central Aeroport of Moscow, is about half an hour walk away from the Kremlin and Red Square. On the way, you will pass Pushkin Square, the location of the first McDonalds fast food restaurant in Russia.

The field became notorious during the coronation of the last Russian Tsar, Nicholas II Romanov in 1894. Nicholas succeeded his father Alexander III at Khodinka field and during the ceremony some two thousand spectators died in the crowd. The Tsar eventually became a strong supporter of aviation and ordered a number Voisin biplanes from France.

In 1910, the famous Russian pilot Boris Rossinsky took off from Khodinka and made the first flight over Moscow. He was generally known as the "Grandfather of Russian Aviation" and reportedly learned to fly from Bleriot in France and, after the revolution in 1917, he joined the Bolsheviks. In the same year, the Flying School of the Imperial Russian Army was formed on this airfield. Between 1910 and 1913 at least twenty-six pilots were successfully trained at the Khodinka school. During this same time frame, the Dux Aviation Works was established, utilizing buildings that had housed a former bicycle factory. In 1914 it became the largest factory in Russia and turned out some 190 aircraft, mostly French-designed Nieuports and Farmans.

When World War I started in 1914, the effort to train new pilots was increased considerably. During the following year, some forty-one officers and fourteen enlisted men received their wings after completing their training at the Imperial Flying School.

Khodinka airfield had a number of crashes and incidents. On 5 June 1919 this Nieuport 24bis crashed during heavy fog into a tower at Khodinka. The pilot, Vladimar Bagdanov was only slightly injured during the incident and later flew again. (Viktor Kulikoi)

The first fighter built by the MiG Design Bureau made its first flight from Khodinka airfield. On 5 April 1940, Arkadij Yekatov took off in the I-200 (MiG-3 prototype) which was subsequently transferred to Zhukovsky airfield for further testing. (Robert Book).

This overall Gray MiG-21MF Fishbed J, White 30 is part of the exhibition at Khodinka. The tactical number was applied as a stencil directly over the camouflage. All three speed brakes are lowered and all weapons pylons have been removed from the aircraft.

In 1917, the British delivered a number of Sopwith 11/2 Strutters, Vickers FB 19s and Be 2Cs as military assistance to Imperial Russia who had joined the war on the Allied side. In early 1917, a group of Royal Air Force instructors under the command of Major J. Valentine arrived at Khodinka to train Russian pilots on the British aircraft.

When the Bolsheviks came to power though a carefully planned and executed Coup d'Etat on 7 November 1917, they inherited a vast empire and a small air force, mainly of British and French design.

In the year following the revolution , the first of the large air parades put on by the Bolsheviks took place over Khodinka in presence of V.I. Lenin. These parades would be held several times a year, one on 1 May (International Labor Day) and another on 7 November (the anniversary of the Revolution).

The Bolsheviks considerably enlarged Khodinka in the post revolutionary years, and the field became Moscow's Central Aeroport. The

field was named Frunze Airfield in honor of the Soviet military theorist and deputy chairman of the Military Revolutionary Council, Mikhail V. Frunze, who died in 1925 under mysterious circumstances.

A number of Soviet types made their first flights from Khodinka. These range form the small R-1 biplane (a copy of the British DH-9) to the gigantic ANT-20 Maxim Gorky. The very first fighter built by the MiG Design bureau, called the I-200, also made its first flight (5 April 1940) from Frunze flown by Arkadij Yekatov.

Both triumph and tragedy were always present at the field. The famous Soviet aviator Valery P. Chkalov died during a crash landing on 15 December 1938, flying a Polikarpov I-180 prototype from Khodinka. He was subsequently buried in the Kremlin wall.

The Dux Aviation Factory at Khodinka, founded under Tzar Nicholas II, became State Aircraft Factory Number One, or GAZ 1 for short. During the interwar years, GAZ 1 turned out Polikarpov I-16s, with the first examples leaving the assembly lines during late 1934. Shortly before the beginning of the Great Patriotic War the factory switched to

The museum's MiG-23S, Blue 22, shortly after its arrival at Khodinka in August of 1992. The wings and stabilizer were missing at this time. This early version of the Flogger was equipped with a Saphire air intercept radar. Evaluation trials with the first production MiG-23S began in May of 1969.

MiG-23S Flogger As were equipped with an R-27F2M-300 power plant. On the later MiG-23M variant the tail surfaces were was relocated rearward, the engine exhaust was shortened and the speed brakes were reinforced. All Flogger versions had a folding ventral fin under the rear fuselage.

7

A MiG-23M Flogger B, Blue 11 (Serial number 09445), shares the grass with a MiG-27 Flogger D. The MiG-23M Flogger B was equipped with a R-29-300 power plant. The bullet shaped drag parachute container at the base of the rudder is open.

This overall air superiority Gray MiG-23M Flogger B, Blue 21, is exhibited without the wing pylons normally found on the Flogger B. The aircraft has a badly faded "Excellent Aircraft" award on the fuselage forward of the tactical number. The FOD guard on the nose wheel has also been removed.

the production of MiG-3 fighters with an average output of about twenty-eight aircraft per day.

MiG-3 and I-16s of the Moscow Air Defense Zone (mainly the 6th Fighter Corps) operated from Khodinka during the battle of Moscow (1941-42) to intercept incoming German bomber raids.

After the war, Khodinka was used as a civil airport. After the opening of Moscow's International Airport (Sheremetjevo), Khodinka lost its importance and was closed to traffic. The Ministry of Civil Aviation; however, still occupies some of the offices and the large military parades on International Labor Day and the Anniversary of the October Revolution are always practiced at Khodinka few days before the event. Located near the field are the MiG and Yakolev Design Bureaus.

As a result of *Glasnost* (July 1991), the Ministry of Aircraft Production and the Ministry of Civil Aviation, began to plan and hold an open exhibition of military equipment, called *Aviatika '91*. Due to its historical importance for Russian aviation, it was decided to open a new aviation museum at Khodinka airfield.

The other museum in the area, the well known Museum of the Air Force at Monino, is closed to the public except for May Day and the Day of Soviet Aviation (19 August). Although most of the aircraft carry full Soviet Air Force markings, few ever saw military service. In fact, most of these aircraft were donated to the museum by the Design Bureaus and the Flight Research Institute "LII" and were mainly used for flight testing and evaluations. As a result these differ in some details

An unusal "eye" nose art was applied on this MiG-23M Flogger B, Blue 11. The Flogger B was equipped with a Saphire-23D-Sh radar. The housing under the nose in front of the nose wheel was for a TP-23 infrared range finder and the three poles in front of the windscreen are the antennas for the Odd Rods IFF system.

from standard production aircraft of the same basic type.

The main exhibits are aircraft and helicopters, but there are also anti-aircraft weapons on display. This exhibit is unprotected and open, as a result it is anticipated that the severe climactic conditions will sooner or later have a negative impact on the condition of the aircraft on display.

Over time the exhibits are changed and various aircraft are rotated through the display. During Aviatika '91, which opened in the Summer of 1991, a Mi-24V Hind E, a Mi-26 Halo, along with a Yak-50 were part of the exhibition. By the Summer of 1992, these aircraft were missing, as was the T-8-15 Frogfoot A prototype. The aircraft participated in the 38th Aero salon at Paris in June of 1989. In 1992, the T-8-15 "Blue 301" was replaced by a Su-25BM "Red 12", a donation of the Sukhoi Design Bureau. In the Summer of 1992, a MiG-23S Flogger A was added to the exhibit.

The open air exhibition was increased by the addition of a tent and a hut with additional exhibits. During this same time frame, some historic aircraft wrecks were added to the exhibit, including a Yak-1M and a Lend-Lease Bell P-39Q. The Bell fighter was lost on a ferry flight to the front over Soviet territory. During the Great Patriotic War, a total of 4,423 P-39 Airacobras were built by Bell at Buffalo for the Soviet Union.

Not only have the exhibits changed since the fall of the Soviet Union, the entrance procedures have also undergone a dramatic change. In 1991, when the Soviet Union was still in existence, the entrance fees could be paid in Rubles, but a year later, Western visitors had to pay the fee in U. S. Dollars. This was not only for the entrance fee, but also for permission to take photographs. This fee varied considerably, on one day the fee was three dollars, later in the week the fee was two dollars, but when the author wanted to take photographs of the Lend-Lease P-39Q, he was not allowed to do so until another fee was paid, in U. S. dollars of course!

With the decline of the Soviet Union, such methods of extracting money from tourists became very popular. During the communist days it was common to be shadowed by a KBG agent, now the chances are much greater to be shadowed by some obscure Russian "aviation enthusiasts" wanting to exchange aircraft equipment, flags, pins, uniforms and books for hard currency. The manager of the museum now sells (as a free enterprise) aviation equipment, such as helmets, flight suits, etc. from a trailer placed within the museum grounds. While you can buy nothing with the Ruble, you can buy almost anything with the Dollar!

Another difference between this and Western museums is that the museum is fitted with loudspeakers that play Western Rock and Pop music (very loud) which is sometimes abruptly followed by softer classic Russian folk music.

The first protoype of the ground attack variant of the Flogger, the MiG-23B Flogger F, which first flew on 20 August 1970 with P.M. Ostapenko at the controls is now on display at the museum. It had the Saphire 2I radar used on the fighter variants replaced by a PrNK *Sokol* (Falcon) navigation and attack system, with a laser range finder mounted behind the window in the nose. The Flogger F could also be used in an air-to-air fighter role with infrared homing missiles.

The first MiG-23B Flogger F ground attack prototype, Green 321 carries White and Black calibration bars on the nose and on the tail for photographic tracking during test flights. In contrast to the standard production MiG-23B, no armor plate was carried on the sides of the fuselage below the cockpit. Additionally, the ECM blisters seen on production aircraft are also missing on the prototype.

A MiG-27 Flogger D, Blue 51 is parked nearby. It differed from the MiG-23BN in a number of ways. The boundary layer intake was not used on the Flogger D and the armament was changed to a single six-barrel GSh-6-30 30ᴍᴍ cannon with 260 rounds. This aircraft has a television camera installed above the wing pylon

This E-155M (MiG-25), Blue 710,captured several world records during 1975 and 1977. On 31 August 1977 the aircraft captured a new altitude record. The aircraft was equipped with two R-15BF-2-300 afterburning turbojet power plants.

This MiG-25RB, Red 55, was a reconnaissance variant of the MiG-25 Foxbat fighter-interceptor. This version had camera windows in the nose and was also equipped with the SRS-4A ELINT system for gathering electronic intelligence.

This is a pre-production MiG-29 Fulcrum fighter. It differed from the production Fulcrum A in that it had a thick antenna mast on the fuselage spine behind the cockpit and a FOD guard in front of the nose wheel.

This MiG-25RB, Red 55, reconnaissance version differed from the interceptor variant in that it was powered by two R-15BD-300 power plants with different engine exhausts, in addition to having the air intercept radar replaced with a camera and ELINT antennas.

This MiG-29 was the fourth of nineteen prototypes/preproduction MiG-29 aircraft built. One of the differences between this aircraft and production MiG-29 Fulcrum As was the ventral fin located just under the horizontal stabilizers.

This Su-7UM Moujik trainer, Red 16, carries a Dark Earth/Dark Green over Light Blue camouflage finish. It was unusual for trainers to carry a tactical camouflage finish. The Su-7UM was the two seat variant of the Su-7 Fitter fighter-bomber.

(Right) The fifth prototype Su-17M-1 carried two non-standard ASO-2V chaff/flare dispensers on the fuselage underside on either side of the ventral fin. Usually two chaff/flare rails with two ASO-2V units were fitted on top of the fuselage on either side of the spine.

This overall Natural Metal Su-17M-1 Fitter, Blue 95, was the fifth Fitter prototype produced by Sukhoi. There were only a few late model Fitters delivered in overall Natural Metal, most came from the factory in a tactical camouflage finish.

This Su-17M-3U, White 99, had the tactical number applied as a White outline against the camouflage finish. This particular Fitter E differed from standard production aircraft in having only two (instead of the normal three) cooling air intakes on the rear fuselage and a different style engine exhaust.

This Su-15 Flagon A, Red 42, has the large radome covering of the *Oriol* (NATO code name Skip Spin) radar displayed on the ramp beside the aircraft. For many years, the Su-15 was the backbone of the PVO (Air Defense) Regiments of the Soviet Air Force.

(Left) The *Oriol* (NATO Code Name Skip Spin) radar worked in the X-band, which is now outdated by more modern look-down/shoot-down systems. The radar scanner antenna was painted in a Chromate Yellow.

The radar antenna of the Skip Scan unit was mounted in the extreme nose of the Su-15 Flagon A. The system was capable of doing both track and scan functions with the single antenna unit.

In August of 1991 this Su-15MT Flagon E was brought in to the museum covered in canvas awaiting re-assembly for display. The aircraft was complete except for the sensor boom above the radome, which was missing. This version was equipped with the Typhoon (Nato Code Name Twin Scan) radar.

The Su-15MT Flagon E after it was re-assembled and placed on display (August 1992). The tactical number, Red 37, had a thin Black outline. The Flagon E differed from the earlier Flagon A in that it had two additional air intakes on the rear fuselage. The Su-15MT was powered by two R-13F-300 power plants.

One difference between the Flagon A and Flagon D was the wing. The Flagon A had a delta shaped wing, while the Flagon D had a wing with a compound sweep. As was standard Soviet practice, no national markings were applied to the wing uppersurfaces. The aircraft was fitted with PU-2-8 missile rails for AA-3 Anab air-to-air missiles (outboard) and APU-62 missile rails for AA-8 Aphids (inboard), both visible just forward of the wing leading edge.

A recording camera was fitted behind the radome of the Su-15 Flagon A along side the SRO-2 Odd Rods three pole IFF antennas. This item was never carried operationally.

This Su-15UT Flagon C, Red 50, is damaged, the balance weight on the stabilizer has been bent upward. The two seat trainer was equipped with the compound sweep wing introduced on all Su-15 versions from the Flagon D onward, and retrofitted to some trainers.

This Su-15 Flagon A, Red 85, is equipped with an additional APU-62 wing pylon to accommodate the R-60MK (AA-8 Aphid) air-to-air missile for close in self-defense. A recording camera has been added under the radome for filming test shoots of the R-60MK or R-98M (AA-3 Anab) air-to-air missiles.

The same aircraft, T-8-15, Blue 301, was transferred to Khodinka when the museum opened in the Summer of 1991. When the aircraft returned from Paris it was involved in various weapons test and service trials aimed at developing the weapons suite for the Frogfoot family.

This Su-27, Red 31, reveals the huge size of the Flanker. Just after this photograph was taken it began to rain heavily; however, it is possible to stand upright under the wing, protecting both us and the camera equipment.

The T-8-15 prototype, Blue 301, on the apron at Zhukovsky-Ramenskoye prior to participation in the Paris Aerosalon. This Frogfoot A was retained by the Sukhoi Design Bureau for test and evaluation work. (Sukhoi Design Bureau)

In the Summer of 1992, the T-8-15 prototype was exchanged for a Su-25BM, Red 12, which had been serving as a target towing aircraft with the AO-17A 30MM twin barreled cannon deleted. No weapons pylons were carried by this Frogfoot A.

Blue 31 was one of a number of pre-production Su-27 Flankers produced by Sukhoi. On this particular aircraft the laser-range finder in front of the canopy was not installed, but the fairing was fitted.

This Blue and Green Yak-38 Forger A, Yellow 60, was fitted with two silver UB-32A thirty-two shot rocket pods on the underwing pylons. This was the sole Naval aircraft at Khodinka. Production of the Forger began during the Summer of 1975.

The cockpit of the Yak-38 Forger A on display at the museum. The overall layout of Russian fighter and ground-attack aircraft are very similar to each other and the equipment is shared between many types.

The Red Excellent Aircraft badge was rather crudely painted on the nose of the Yak-38 Forger A, Yellow 60. This entire aircraft had a very weathered appearance.

The folding wing tip of the Yak-38 Forger A allows more aircraft to be carried on Soviet ships. The aircraft was armed with two thirty-two shot silver UB-32A rocket pods that held S-5 unguided air-to-ground rockets. The Yak-38 is fitted with two R-27V-300 cruise engines and two RD-36-35 lift engines.

This Mi-2, Yellow 03, carries an early non-standard camouflage of Olive Drab, Dark Green and Yellow. Although the Hoplite was designed in the Soviet Union, the entire production run was done in Poland.

For some unknown reason this Mi-2, Yellow 03, had been painted in phony U.S. Air Force markings on the tail boom. Later these markings were overpainted with the camouflage finish, and now they are bleeding through overspray.

This Mi-24A Hind A, Red 33, represented the first version of the helicopter gunship and was equipped with a front section armored greenhouse cockpit. The aircraft was normally armed with a 12.7MM machine gun in the nose (which is missing on this gunship).

This Mi-24V Hind E was on display during the Summer of 1991, but was missing a year later. The Hind carried the clover-leaf camouflage pattern, typical for early Hind Ds and Es. Some of the Green clover leaf pattern is repainted with Light Blue. The aircraft is carrying the later style rocket pods that have replaced the earlier UB-32 pods in most Hind units.

The Mi-26 Halo helicopter remained at Khodinka only a short period. The Mi-26 is the largest helicopter in current service anywhere in the world. The aircraft is also used by India and the Russian civil airline Aeroflot.

A Yak-50 acrobatic aircraft of the para-military orginization. DOSAAF was on display at Khodinka during the Summer of 1991, but a year later the Yak-50 was missing. Typical for DOSAAF aircraft, full Soviet Air Force markings are carried on the aircraft.

This Lend-Lease Bell P-39Q Airacobra was lost during a ferry flight to the front over Soviet territory and was salvaged. The aircraft was transferred to Khodinka for storage during the Summer of 1992. Only the lower propeller blades are bent, indicating that the crash landing was made with the engine shut down and the propeller not moving. The Allison V-1710-85 12-cylinder engine behind the cockpit is visible, this rear mounted engine was one of the distinctive features of the P-39.

Zhukovsky (Ramenskoye)

During the Cold War period, the Test and Experimental Center at Zhukovsky was one of the most heavily guarded sites in the Soviet Union. In recent times most of the new aircraft, both civil and military, were tested from Zhukovsky and many made their first flights from this field.

Located some thirty-five miles to the southeast of the center of Moscow, the test center is better known in the West as Ramenskoye. The name; however, was an American-creation based on incorrect information. Part of the main runway passes a railway station named Ramenskoye and the name was picked by U.S. intelligence to name the adjacent test center at the beginning of the Cold War. One of the main sources for location names within the Soviet Union were in fact maps captured from the German Wehrmacht during the Second World War. These came from the huge amount of intelligence material provided by the Fremde Heere Ost Department of the Wehrmacht.

To the Russians, the airfield complex is known as Zhukovsky, named after Nikolai Jegorovich Zhukovsky, regarded by many, including Lenin, as the "founding father" of Russian aviation.

In 1904, he founded the country's first aerodynamic institute and on 1 December 1918 he established the Central Hydrodynamic Institute (TSAGI) near Ramenskoye. A year after Nikolai Jegorovich's death in March of 1921, the site was named Zhukovsky.

The entire Zhukovsky complex is very large. It has two hard surfaced runways, one of them being more than five kilometers, making it the world's largest concrete runway. Even after the end of the Communist era, the base is very well protected in order to keep its secrets intact.

Only one other base has a tighter bolt of security. This is the Test and Experimental Center of the Air Force NII-VVS in the Astrochan area. NII-VVS is responsible for combat testing of new aircraft and weapons systems, while Zhukovsky is responsible to investigating the flight characteristics of new aircraft and to check if the type meets the intended technical requirements issued by the Ministry of Aircraft Production.

Zhukovsky is under the control of the Flight Research Institute (LII), and the complex is divided into branches and a number of the hangars are allocated to the various design bureaus housed at the base.

Further hangars and buildings accommodate the TSAGI, the Gromov Flight Research institute and parts of the All Union Institute for Aviation Material (VIAM).

The hangars and offices of the Design Bureaus are lined up on both sides of the main entrance, Yakovlev at the front, followed by Tupolev, Sukhoi, MiG and Iljushin.

Despite the large size of the base, there are only about sixty aircraft currently based there for flight research and tests by the Design Bureaus and the LII. A further forty aircraft are in non-airworthy condition and awaiting scrapping or will be stored by the Design Bureaus in the allo-

Many aircraft prototypes were test flown at Zhukovsky which did not develop beyond the early prototype stage; such as the I-207, a biplane fighter designed by the team of A.A. Borovkov and I.F. Florov. It was powered by a single 850 hp M-62 radial air-cooled engine. (Viktor Kulikov)

The French-built Dewoitine D-510 was purchased by a Soviet Purchasing Commission. It was test flown at Zhukovsky with no national markings. The pattern of the runway blocks was typical for Soviet airfields. (Yefim Gordon)

cated areas. There are also a number of wrecked aircraft near the hangars assigned to the Design Bureaus and on both sides of the main runways.

The huge complex also has housing for the test pilots and their families with a complete infrastructure, making it basically a small town, cut off from the outside world in order to guarantee security. There are no less than five well guarded entrances placed around the base.

The heart of the test center was and still is the complex operated by TSAGI, with its huge wind-tunnels, some large enough to hold complete aircraft. The Soviet aviation industry has traditionally put great emphasis on aerodynamics; in fact in many successful designs, aerodynamics made up for shortcomings in Soviet power plants.

The Soviet Union has led the way in the development of wind tunnels. In 1923, the center opened the largest, for its time, wind tunnel in the world. It had a diameter of six meters (19.7 feet) and a length of fifty meters (164 feet). Most of the TSAGI buildings were built during 1935 and in 1939, a completely new T-101 wind tunnel was built. This was so huge that it was possible to test a complete twin engined bomber of the Pe-2 class within the tunnel. More than 10,000 scientists, engineers and workers are employed by the TSAGI.

TSAGI is now offering its expertise and facilities to the West. For instance, the Transonic Wind Tunnel T-128, which has a square cross section of 2.75 x 2.75 m (9 feet) and a length of 8 meters (26 feet) with a range of Mach numbers between 0.15 and 1.7 Mach. Also available is the highly capable *ARGON* CAD (Computer Aided Design) used for aerodynamic research, and a modern vacuum chamber for thermal strength testing. Boeing has become the first American company to sign an agreement with the TSAGI covering joint research projects and the use of the Institute's wind tunnels.

The Gromov Flight Research Institute is offering its Il-76LL (SSSR-06188) flying lab for inflight tests and development of gas-turbine

Italian-built Fiat CR-32 was captured by the Republicans during the Spanish Civil War and was subsequently taken by ship to the Soviet Union, where an evaluation program was flown at Zhukovsky. This aircraft was of particular interest, since it saw combat against the Polikarpov I-15 and I-16. (Robert Book)

This German Heinkel He-51 biplane fighter was also captured during the Spanish Civil War and test flown. The aircraft was overall Silver dope with Red trim and had Soviet national markings applied to the fuselage and wings. (Dr. Volker Koos)

engines of various types up to 25,000 kgst (55,114 lbst). The Il-76LL is equipped with a wide range of test and measuring facilities, including magnetic storage, oscilloscopes and visual indicators of different types, plus a TV-system. There is also an on-board digital computer system with a variety of peripherals, making it possible to process test data in real time. The maximum flight altitude of the II-76LL for test flights is 12,000 meters (39,370 feet) and the maximum speed is 600 km/h (372 mph).

During the communist era, the procedure was to transfer the pattern aircraft, after all changes, directly into production at state factories. While it was most common in the early days that the new design made its first fight near the manufacturing plant and was then transferred to a test facility for State Acceptance. Now most aircraft are transferred by road to the Research Institute and then reassembled by factory specialists and prepared for flight. This procedure allows far greater security. Following successful factory test trials, the aircraft will be handed over for State Acceptance trials to the Flight Research Institute (LII) which will determine its suitability for mass production. These trials, for both civil and military aircraft, are all conducted by LII test pilots during which time the prototypes remain at Zhukovsky.

After they have met the governments handling and performance requirements, combat aircraft will be transferred to the Air Force's Science and Experimental Institute (NII-VVS) in the Astrochan area for weapons trials.

The Flight Research Institute (LII) also tested and evaluated a large number of foreign types. During the interwar years, a number of Italian, French and German aircraft were legally purchased and subsequently tested at Zhukovsky.

The Tu-2 Paravan was a cable cutting version of the Tu-2 bomber. A twenty foot long cone was installed from which steel wires led to the modified wingtips, which held the cable cutters. Tests with the Tu-2 Paravan were conducted during 1944. (Robert Book)

During the Spanish Civil War, some Italian and German aircraft were captured by the Republicans and subsequently shipped by boat to the Soviet Union. Flight trials were undertaken with a Fiat CR-32, a Messerschmitt Bf 109, a Heinkel He 51 and a Heinkel He 111.

Further German aircraft were test flown by the Flight Research Institute during the Great Patriotic War, some damaged aircraft were rebuilt from parts of other aircraft and subsequently tested as well.

When England and the United States granted Land-Lease help to

When the first Bell P-400 arrived as Lend-Lease aid, the aircraft were assembled and test flown at Zhukovsky with their original RAF markings. This Airacobra I (serial AH628) had a 20MM Hispano Mk I cannon in the nose. (Yefim Gordon)

This Lend-Lease Bell P-39Q-25-BE (44-32467) Airacobra was equipped with a recording camera fitted on top of the canopy frame and a Soviet developed anti-spin parachute under the port wing. Normally, the large White roundels around the Red star were over-painted with Green. (Yefim Gordon)

19

A Bell P-63A-7-BE (42-69188) Kingcobra during its evaluation with the Flight Test Institute. The aircraft markings were unusual, since the White roundel (applied at the Bell factory) was overpainted on the fuselage, but was retained on the wing undersurfaces. A feature found on Kingcobras supplied to the Russians was a DF (Direction Finding) loop antenna which was on the fuselage spine behind the canopy. (Yefim Gordon)

The Flight Research Institute also rebuilt captured aircraft during the Second World War. This particular Focke Wolf Fw 190 was restored to flying condition with spare parts from various other aircraft. The hangar where the Fw 190 was stored is located near the main entrance and today houses the engine test branch of the Flight Research Institute. (Yefim Gordon)

Russia, at least one aircraft of each type was tested at Zhukovsky. As in the case of Soviet built aircraft, for each foreign type the State Acceptance test had to made.

During late 1941 the Soviet Union desperately needed any fighter and bomber aircraft they could get to face the advancing Wehrmacht and, as a result, these aircraft were immediately allocated to front-line units while the State Acceptance was still in progress. Some Soviet developed detail improvements on Lend-Lease aircraft were also tested at Zhukovsky.

After the Second World War, intact German and Japanese aircraft found within Moscow's sphere of influence were taken to Zhukovsky for flight test and evaluation by the Flight Research Institute and the results of these evaluations often found their way into Soviet designs.

Through the years TSAGI built up an extraordinary interesting sample collection of Soviet and foreign aircraft, which were placed in a hangar at Zhukovsky. Besides all the major combat aircraft of the Second World War, a number of Lend-Lease aircraft and captured German aircraft were also on exhibit. According to unconfirmed information, most of these aircraft were broken up in the 1970s.

The site drew considerable interest from the United States and other NATO countries and there were some U.S. reconnaissance satellites focused on Ramenskoye. When a new type was detected during flight testing, it was given the designation RAM (for Ramenskoye) with a suffix, since it was hard to determine from space the aircraft's designer. For an example, when the Su-27 was detected during 1977. it was allocated the designation RAM K before it was given its NATO name Flanker A.

But through the years the Soviet Union developed very effective counter-measure against the U.S. satellites. It is a fact that a satellite cannot monitors a location 24 hours a day and what the Soviets did was simply to delay all testing activities until after the satellites had passed over Zhukovsky.

The success of the Soviet countermeasure system was based on ground stations and aerial tracking of satellites by modified Il-76 Candid and Il-86 Camber aircraft. These particular aircraft all carry Aeroflot markings, but are easy to distinguish from standard production aircraft in having a large hump on top of the fuselage and a number of additional antennas.

Once the satellites were traced it was relatively easy to estimate when the birds were over the test site. Since 1977 when a computer error resulted in the West getting photos of the MiG-29, Su-25 and Su-27, no other new combat aircraft were caught out in the open.

Part of TSAGI's sample collection, which included, besides famous Soviet aircraft, captured German aircraft. In addition, the collection also had a number of American and British aircraft supplied under Lend-Lease. The Bf-109G-2 was followed by a Bell P-400 Airacobra I and a North American Mustang Mk I. Although the Mustang is carrying early style USAAF markings, shipment of the Mustang I was made out of England from RAF stocks. (Yefim Gordon)

This heavily modified German Junkers Ju-352 was used an a testbed for various engines. The nose boom was considerably enlarged and a number of test and recording instruments were installed in the aircraft to monitor engine performance. (Viktor Kulikov)

This experimental jet, the I-215, was one of the many unsucessful Soviet first generation jet-fighter designs. It was similar in appearance to the British Gloster Meteor, a much more successful design. (Viktor Kulikov)

The main runway at Zhukovsky is some five km long, making it one of the longest runways in the world. Trucks mounting converted jet-engines are used to blast away the snow and ice from the runway in order to keep the base open regardless of the weather. (Viktor Kulikov)

As an additional security measure, the Soviets painted new aircraft or new versions of existing types in such a way that they resembled already well known types, additionally in some cases part of the evaluation envelope performed by the Flight Research Institute was done in places which were not under satellite observation.

A good example how tight the security measures for new types was in the Soviet Union is the Il-102, a competing design against the Su-25. The two seat ground attack aircraft first flew in 1978 from Zhukovsky, but no information of its existence or a satellite picture ever leaked to the West.

According to unofficial sources, there were at least twelve different types flown in the recent years without the West gaining any knowledge of their existence, moreover there are at least five completely new designs in flight test at Zhukovsky.

The new Yeltsin government shows very little intention towards an open "Glasnost" policy, at least where the development of new aircraft is concerned. While the budget cuts affect aircraft production, there is no restriction on money for development of new military equipment. Additionally, just like in the good old Communist tradition, this will all continue under tight security.

Perhaps one reason for the development of new military aircraft is that the new Russian government wants to prevent its highly qualified designers and engineers from emigrating to the West or into one of the newly formed CIS countries.

In early 1992, the Yeltsin Government announced that a Russian aviation exhibition would be held in Ramenskoye. This was it first indica-

A pre-production MiG-29 Fulcrum rests on a three point cradle after being installed for aerodynamic testing in the huge wind tunnel at Zhukovsky in September of 1991. TSAGI now offers the use of these test facilities to the West and Boeing was the first American company to sign a contract for a joint research project. (Steve Zaloga)

One of the MiG-29 Fulcrums used by the Flight Research Institute for engine tests. The antenna covering under the rudder was not standard fitting on service Fulcrums and probably is a cover for telemetry antennas. This is an early production aircraft identified by the centerline ILS antenna under the nose. (Viktor Kulikov)

tion of a remarkable turning point in Russian policy. For years Zhukovsky was one of the most secure spots in the entire Soviet Union. In reality, Mosaeroshow '92, held between 10 and 16 August 1992 was nothing more than a propaganda demonstration to get the world to believe that the Yeltsin government was on a democratic course. The exhibition was held on the shorter of the two parallel runways, while the

One of the Su-27 Flankers, Red 05, which belongs to the Flight Research Institute (LII). This Flanker does not have a laser range finder installed in front of the canopy as is standard on production Flanker Bs. On the aircraft's dorsal spine, behind the antenna mast, is another small antenna, which is also a non-standard fitting. This aircraft was later demonstrated in the United States. (Viktor Kulikov)

rest of the Zhukovsky complex was still off limits. In order to prevent an unwanted unveiling of new aircraft to Western enthusiasts the government took special measures to control crowds and access to the base. A few days before the show, all aircraft that were considered too sensitive were moved off base to the NII-VVS test base at Astrochan and to other locations. A number of smaller fighter sized aircraft were put in specially guarded hangars far away from the actual show area. Once the show ended, the aircraft were flown back and Zhukovsky had kept most of its secrets from the Western world!

During the airshow hundreds of soldiers and Militia (Soviet Police) secured the base and closely watched that no one "got lost" or was taking photographs of forbidden areas. There was a long line of many different types, but with the exception of the Il-102, all had been previously known in the West. The quantity and quality of the aircraft displayed, however, was an impressive demonstration of the current state of the Russian aviation industry.

This Su-27IB, Blue 42, on take off from Zhukovsky, is one of two pro-
totypes conducting evaluation flights from this base. The Su-27IB
Flanker has been designed as a shore-based attack plane for the
Russian Navy. (A.A. Zirnov)

This An-12, Red 15, (with a thin White outline around the number) is
equipped with various antennas and a bubble shaped round observation window on the fuselage side. This Cub was used for
Electronic Countermeasures (ECM) trials. The front of the propeller
spinners was painted in Light Blue. (Viktor Kulikov)

This An-12 (6344510), Red 10, is equipped with a dorsal mounted airfoil, an undernose radome and a camera pod. It is used by TSAGI for
de-icing trials. The circular device in front of the airfoil is used to
pump out a water spray to test the ice buildup on the airfoil, a second spray device is towed behind the aircraft to spray water on aircraft flying in formation behind the An-12 for engine icing tests.
(Viktor Kulikov)

This An-12 (6344510), Red 10, has the normal tail gun armament
replaced by a camera installation. The aircraft also has a number of
additional antennas and sensor blisters fitted on the fuselage spine
and sides. (Viktor Kuljkov)

This is the Il-76LL used by the Gromov Institute as a flying laborato-
ry. The test engine is always fitted on the port inboard pylon. In this
case, the aircraft is fitted with an experimental turboprop engine.
(Viktor Kulikov)

The Type 976 is a variant of the A-50 Mainstay AWACS aircraft used by the Flight Research Institute to control and investigate flight testing of prototypes. There were three Type 976 aircraft allocated to the LII, including this aircraft serial SSSR-76453. (Viktor Kulikov)

This An-12 (Serial Number 8345902) has a modified tail section for use in ejection seat flight tests. Pods on the wing tip and the rear fuselage carry cameras and other recording instrumentation. The two Black bar antennas on top of the fuselage are also a non-standard fitting. (Viktor Kabanov)

This Tu-134A (SSSR-65907) was modified to serve as the MiG-29 radar testbed. It was usually parked on a hardstand at Zhukovsky when not flying radar test missions.

A complete MiG-29 Fulcrum nose section, housing its RLPK-29 radar was grafted onto the nose section of the Tu-134A radar test bed. Normally a canvas sheet is kept over the radome to hide it from above.

There are three Tu-144 Supersonic Transports (SSTs) in storage at Zhukovsky, including SSSR-77113. Although they appear to be in good condition, these Soviet Concord competitors are no longer airworthy and it is doubtful that they will ever fly again.

(Left) This overall Medium Gray Il-62M (SSSR-86561) carries a large White antenna on the upper fuselage. It is believed that this is a presidential aircraft fitted with a wide variety of communications equipment. It is no longer airworthy and is in storage at Zhukovsky.

One of the Type 976s, the civil version of the A-60 Mainstay AWACS aircraft. These differ from the military variant in that they have a glazed nose section and lack air refueling equipment. The aircraft has been parked with the thrust reversers on each engine in the full open position, even though there are Red engine covers in place over each intake.

This MiG-23S Flogger A, Blue 22, sets on the ramp at Khodinka shortly after its arrival for inclusion in the museum with the outer wing panels and horizontal stabilizer missing.

This Ye-155M, Blue 710, broke the world altitude record on 31 August 1977. The new record was 37,650 meters (123,523.6 feet) which still stands today. The Ye-155 was a variant of the MiG-25.

Two of the Sukhoi products on display are this Su-25BM, Red 12, and a Su-27, Red 31. Both aircraft were donated to the museum by the Sukhoi Design Bureau. The tent in the background houses a photographic exhibit of Soviet aviation in the Second World War.

This early Mi-24A Hind A, Red 33, on display at Khodinka has the 12.7MM machine gun, normally carried in the nose, deleted. The Hind A was the first version of the Hind to go into widespread service.

The forth pre-production MiG-29, Blue 04, parked on the ramp at Khodinka.The ventral fin and the FOD guard on the nose wheel were typical features found on pre-production Fulcrum As.

This MiG-23M, Blue 11, has an eye painted on the nose. Parked along side it are a MiG-27 Flogger D and another MiG-23M. These aircraft remain in the open the year around and it is expected that the harsh Russian winters will soon have a negative impact on the display.

A Su-15 Flagon A is displayed with its large radome removed from the aircraft and placed beside it to give a good view of the *Oriol* (Skip Spin) radar dish and other equipment inside the nose. The Su-15 was armed with the R-98 (AA-3) Anab air to-air missile.

The two space tracking Il-76MDs on the ramp at Ramenskoye. These aircraft differ from standard Il-76 Candids in a number of ways, the windows in the nose are faired over and a large sensor housing is mounted on the upper fuselage. The aircraft in the foreground is Il-76MD SSSR-76450, followed by the second aircraft SSSR-76451 and a standard Candid SSSR-76830 in the background.

One of the two modified Il-76 (SSSR-76450) used for space tracking. These aircraft all carry Aeroflot civil airline markings. This was intended as a sort of camouflage to hide the true purpose of the aircraft from Western observers.

This Tu-154 (SSSR-85055) is stored at Zhukovsky without its engines. Like so many other aircraft on the field it is non-airworthy and has been cannibalized of usable parts and now awaits its final fate.

The entire Zhukovsky complex is littered with junk; wrecked aircraft; discarded drop tanks and other items. The aircraft in the background is a Tu-154 (SSSR-85055) that was once used for flight testing before being stripped of its engines and other equipment.

The Tupolev Design Bureau has its own area at Zhukovsky. On the right is a Tu-95MS Beat H and next to it is a Tu-154 fuselage with traces of the old Aeroflot markings. The Tu-160 Blackjack is under repair with the vertical stabilizer missing.

The Flight Research Iistitute LII has allocated each design bureau a number of hangars. Tupolev, a builder of large bombers has received most of the larger hangers. Most of the buildings were built around 1935. A Tu-22M and a Tu-134BU modified with a Backfire nose section are parked in front of the hangars.

(Above/Below) This Yak-40 (SSSR-88238) was fitted with six ASO-2I chaff/flare dispenser rails. One mounted under each wing glove and four units placed under the tail. This modification was developed for Yak-40s serving in Afghanistan in order to give them protection from Stinger surface-to-air missiles. The aircraft also has a bubble observers window and Odd Rods IFF antennas on the nose.

An overall Light Gray Tu-22M Backfire on the apron at Zhukovsky taxies to its hardstand in the Tupolev Design Bureau area. This Tu-22M was retained by the Tupolev OKB for use in various test programs.

(Right) The only really new type introduced during Mosaeroshow '92 was the Il-102 two seat attack aircraft, an unsuccessful competitor to the Su-25 Frogfoot. Prior to the show, no information of its existence had ever leaked to the West.

(Below/Right)The cockpit of the Il-102 featured a HUD display and a K-36 ejection seat. The cockpit layout is generally similar to other ground attack and fighter aircraft in the Soviet inventory.

The rear turret featured a twin barreled cannon which was remotely operated by the gunner from his cockpit. The small device next to the cannon is a television sighting system for the gun.

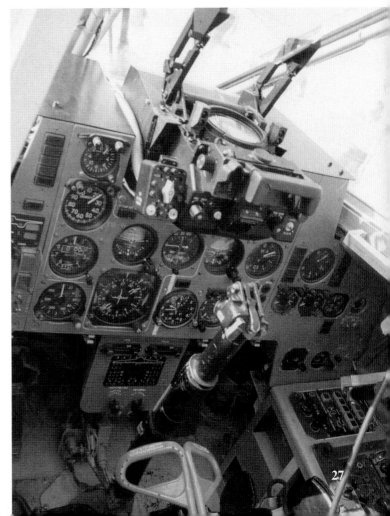

27

This Il-62M on the ramp at Ramenskoye during the Summer of 1992 was used for VIP flights and is equipped with a number of antenna fairings on top of the fuselage. All government aircraft carried Aeroflot markings even though they were never operated by the state airline.

A line-up of L-39C Albatros trainers of the Soviet Aerobatic Team. The aircraft assigned to this team carry either two or three digit tactial numbers. The aircraft in the foreground is L-39 (Serial 931510) White 11.

This An-32 was recently repainted in United Nations colors and given the registration UN 975. This aircraft previously flew for the Soviet Air Force before it was donated to the UN for service in the Balkans.

This Aero L-39C, Blue 001, of the Soviet Aerobatic Team is the only one of the team to receive a special color scheme. All the other L-39s carry standard Soviet Air Force camouflage and markings.

A number of aircraft on the engine test area of the Flight Research Institute ramp at Ramenskoye. The aircraft in the foreground is a standard Yak-40, followed by an United Nations An-32 and an An-12.

This Tu-95LL Bear was used as an engine testbed. The experimental engine was fitted under the fuselage in place of the usual bomb bay. The large tunnel to led the exhaust away from the aircraft during ground test runs of the engine.

This Soviet Air Force Tu-134, Red 01, carries a special container under the fuselage, probably to house electronic intelligence equipment. There is also a bank of sensors on the fuselage in front of the wing.

This modified Il-76TD (SSSR-76451) had a large sensor fairing above the cockpit and also carried a number of other sensors and antennaes, including a sensor pod under each wing. This Candid is used for tracking Western satellites over Ramenskoye.

This An-2 was formerly operated by DOSAAF, although it carried full Soviet Air Force markings and a Yellow tactical number (05). The An-2 in the background carries the new Russian White/Blue/Red fin flash

An An-24B, Red 01, warms up its AI-23VT turboprop engines at Tushino during August of 1991. This aircraft was mainly used for VIP flights.

A Polish-built An-2TD, Yellow 03, returns to its hardstand at Tushino after having completed a paradrop run for some sky divers over the area. All of the An-2s belong to DOSAAF.

This An-26 civil cargo aircraft (SSSR-01208) and the Air Force An-24B, Red 01, both carry the new Russian White/Blue/Red fin flash on the vertical fin. The aircraft were at Tushino during the Summer of 1992.

Ground crewmen mount one of the two auxiliary fuel tanks on the fuselage of a Soviet Air Force Mi-2 Hoplite. The total fuel capacity of the two tanks is 470 liters (124 gallons).

A camouflaged Soviet Air Force Mi-8T Hip C assault helicopter, Yellow 79, shares the grass field at Tushino Air Base during the Summer of 1991 with Polish-built An-2D biplane transports.

This ex-Vietnamese F-5E (73-00878) was delivered under very tight security to the Czechs for evaluation during 1981. In addition, the Czechs also received two AIM-9 Sidewinder missiles and some ground support equipment. (Otakar Saffek)

This was the first MiG-21UM, Black 23 85, destroyed by technicians of *Elbe Flugzeugwerke GmbH* at Dresden on 22 September 1992. All usable equipment had been stripped from the aircraft and the skeleton was cut into pieces by a cutting torch. (Andreas Scbutz)

This partially unpainted Tu-160 Blackjack bomber was retained by Tupolev and based at Zhukovsky for use in flight test programs. According to Russian sources, the Blackjack is not well liked by Soviet Air Force crews.

This Tu-95LL was used as an engine testbed with the engine being tested mounted under the fuselage in the area formerly taken up by the bomb bay. A large duct leading from the exhaust area of the engine to a noise suppressor is visible under the aircraft.

This overall White An-32 (UN 976) was donated to the United Nations for use in the former Yugoslavia. The type designation "AN-32" is in Cyrillic while the lettering "United nations' is in English.

The Tu-95LL was converted from an early Bear A bomber version. There are currently three Bear airframes being used for engine testing. The Bear is powered by four Kuznetsov NK-12MV turboprops driving contra-rotating propellers. The engine was originally developed by German scientists in the Soviet Union.

This Tu-134A, tactical number Red 01, on the ramp at Zhukovsky is a rather unusual aircraft. It has been modified with a sensor panel on the fuselage side and a pod under the fuselage. The purpose of these modifications is unknown, but they are most likely involved with electronic intelligence gathering.

The Tu-134A, Red 01, has a canvas covered pod mounted on the centerline and what appears to be an antenna array on the fuselage side. The pod appears to be electronic in nature, perhaps either ECM or ELINT.

The flight line of L-39 aerobatic team after performing an impressive demonstration over Zhukovsky. Only one of the L-39s carries special Red and White markings. There were a number of aircraft with two digit tactical numbers, while others had three digit tactical numbers. The second Albatros in line, White 38, has a White tactical number with a thin Red outline and carries an Excellent Aircraft badge on the nose

A Czech built Aero L-39, White 108, on the taxiway of Zhukovsky. Usually, three digit tactical numbers are only issued to training regiments. This aircraft is part of the Russian L-39 Aerobatic Team that was performing a show over Zhukovsky.

This canvas covered MiG-21 Fishbed was once used as a chase aircraft for other aircraft involved in flight test work at Zhukovsky. The MiG-21 was not airworthy and was in long term storage. The aircraft in the background are Yak-40s.

This former Soviet Air Force overall Gray An-12 Cub turboprop transport now carries the civil registration SSSR-13321. The Soviet fin flash on the fin is of a non-standard style. The aircraft in the background is a Il-76 Candid (SSSR-76756).

31

All former East German Air Force MiG-29s now carry a two tone Gray air superiority camouflage scheme and full West German markings. This MiG-29 Fulcrum A, Black 20+16 once flew as Red 699 with the East Germans. The Black numbers have a thin White outline. (Jenz Schymura)

This Fitter K the 77th Fighter Bomber Regiment (Serial 25714) Red 546 on the apron of Laage-Kronskamp carried these special marking to mark the last flights of the East German Air Force prior to the reunification of the two German republics. (E. Prell)

Red 546 was later repainted with West German Air Force markings and given the West German registration, Black 25+07. (E. Prell)

This MiG-21MF Fishbed J (Serial 8615) was given its special camouflage by ground crewmen from the 2nd Squadron of the 1st Fighter Regiment. The wing glove and the braking parachute container were Red and the cockpit was outlined in Yellow. (Jens Schymura)

This MiG-23ML Flogger G (Serial 0390324255), Red 488, was the last Flogger of the 3rd Fighter Regiment. It was flown from the regiment's home base Peenemunde to the Laage-Kronskamp storage depot for final disposal. These special markings were applied for a photo session on 1 July 1991. (Eckhardt Prell)

With the rear portion of the engine cover removed and the speed brakes in the deployed position this MiG-23ML Flogger G (Serial 0390324031, Black 20 31) rests on a hardstand at Laage-Kronskamp in April of 1993. It flew once as Red 563 with the 1st Squadron of the 9th Fighter Regiment. (Eckhardt Prell)

This MiG-21PFM, Black 22+02, was the last Fishbed of the 1st Fighter Regiment to be ferried from its former home base at Holzdorf to Drewitz storage depot. The canvas cover over the cockpit was borrowed from another MiG-21PFM coded Black 22+04. (Eckhardt Prell)

This MiG-23MF (Serial 0390213299) was once assigned to the 9th Fighter Regiment, Heinrich Rau, in August of 1978 as Red 577. It was flown to Laage-Kronskamp Air Base for storage with the West German registration Black 20-02. A number of the maintenance hatches have been removed. (Eckhardt Prell)

This MiG-21PFM once carried the code Red 441 when it was stationed at Holzdorf Air Base. Only the upper surfaces were painted White, the undersurfaces remained in the original Light Blue used when the aircraft was camouflaged. The centerline drop tank has been removed. (Werner Greppmeir)

Tushino Airfield

Tushino Airfield, on the outskirts of Moscow, has played host for many important air shows and air displays during the interwar and post-war period. Shortly after Comrade Iosif Stalin came to power he ruthlessly pushed forward a program of industrialization. Tushino Airfield was often selected in the interwar period as the site to introduce the new aviation achievements to the public.

From 1929 onward, the field was the location for the Central Flying Technical School of the Society for Assistance to Defense, Aviation and Chemistry Osoaviakhim. Pilots and technicians belonging to a number of different aviation specialties were trained here. Additionally, the base was selected (in May of 1933) as the site of a parachute school.

The number of different flying clubs, glider stations and parachute towers was constantly increasing in the Soviet Union. As a result it became necessary to establish a center, where the experience gained from the various civil aviation activities and sport aviation could be organized and where a central record archive could be set up.

The Central Flying Club was formed at Tushino and by special resolution this club was officially adopted by government and party organizations. New buildings were erected and the airfield was developed and enlarged. According to official propaganda, many Komsomol (Communist Youth Organization) members of the Moscow branch worked on the field. It is also believed that during the re-building of the base political prisoners were used to perform forced labor.

The main construction of hangars, buildings and flying club buildings was finished by the beginning of 1935. On 11 March 1935 the Central Flying Club was officially dedicated. It comprised a learning center, a training squadron forming three detachments, a separate crop spraying detachment and a special detachment.

On 12 July 1935 the first aviation parade was held and Iosif Stalin and other leaders of the party and government were present. Such parades became a standard and were held at Tushino airfield every year, becoming a peoples holiday.

During the "Day of Aviation" parade on 18 August 1935 the new Polikarpov I-16 fighter was demonstrated to the public for the first time, when a formation five I-16s was flown over Tushino. The I-16 entered Soviet Air Force service the same year and was introduced to the public some three months earlier during the May Day celebration over Moscow's Red Square.

During the early years the Central Flying Club was named after the first secretary of the Youth Communist League Central Committee, A. Kosarev. Later, during the Stalinist repression he was executed and the

The Yak-15 jet fighter was developed from the earlier piston engined Yak-3 of the Second World War. It was demonstrated for the first time to the public during the Aviation Parade over Tushino on 18 August 1946. (Zbigniew Luranc)

The other jet powered fighter demonstrated to startled Western military attaches at Tushino was the MiG-9. The Soviet Air Force issued no information regarding either the manufacturer or the type designation during the demonstration, leading to much speculation in the West. (Andrzei Morgala)

Central Flying Club was renamed after Valery Chkalov, the well known Soviet test pilot. Even after the end of Communism in Russia, the name of this great Soviet aviator remains.

In August of 1935, the gigantic ANT-20 Maxim Gorky, an eight-engined propaganda aircraft, the largest aircraft in the world, was shown over Tushino. For the flight it carried forty-four people including some TSAGI engineers. During the demonstration, a Polikarpov I-5 fighter, flown by Nikolai Blagin, collided with the ANT-20, and both aircraft crashed.

On 18 August 1937, the Day of Soviet Aviation, was attended by nearly one million Soviet citizens to view an exhibition of aircraft, the most highly touted product of Soviet industry and the proudest arm of Soviet military might. Soviet State Aircraft Factories had produced 4,435 aircraft that year and the Muscovites were being given a chance to see the Red Air Force put the aircraft through a number of maneuvers.

The show was dazzling, the climax came when dozens of aircraft moved gracefully in and out of formation that spelled 'Lenin, Stalin and USSR. For a grand finale, the formation took the shape of a five pointed star, symbol of the Bolshevik Revolution.

At the beginning of the Great Patriotic War, the Central Flying Club was evacuated from Moscow, first to Golitsino and then to Vladimirovka near Stalingrad. In 1942, during the fierce battles near Stalingrad, it moved to Kazan. The few aviation specialists who remained at Tushino managed to instruct some 350 pilots during the war year, in addition, some 2,000 parachutists and 350 glider pilots were also trained.

After the Great Patriotic War, Tushino continued its importance as a demonstration airfield. During the celebration of the Day of Aviation on 18 August 1946 the first two Soviet jet-powered fighter aircraft were shown to the public, the Yak-15 and the MiG-9. This event at Tushino led to the creation of the USAF number system to identify new Soviet aircraft. This system came about due to the fact that these aircraft were all shown to the public without any designation or manufacturer. The Yak-15 became Type 1 and the MiG-9 became the Type 2 in USAF parlance. Later, in mid-1955 the USAF found the numeral code a little bit difficult to handle and dropped this code-system in favor of the NATO ASCC name reporting system.

During the early stage of the Cold War period, Tushino was, as the site of the May Day Celebrations, one of the only sources for Western military attaches and observers to obtain information on new Soviet hardware. As a result, beside thousands of Soviet citizens, many diplomats from NATO and neutral Western oriented countries attended the air demonstrations.

In June of 1955, the MiG-19 Farmer, the first supersonic fighter to enter Soviet service was introduced at Tushino. A year later, on 24 June

This Olive Green over Light Blue An-2TD Colt biplane transport, Yellow 05, was built in Poland. The two antenna fairings on the underside of the rear fuselage is a standard feature on all PZL-built An-2s.

1956, the prototype of the MiG-21 series, the Ye-5, was presented alongside the Yak-25 Flashlight and perhaps one of the most mysterious Soviet bombers in the mid-1950s, the Tu-98 Backfin.

The presence of these aircraft, which were all previously unknown in the West, drew a lot of speculation. This was the last show of its kind at Tushino during this decade. The 1957 Aviation Day was canceled and the 1958 event comprised a fly-by of only civil aircraft.

In the early 1990s, Tushino was surrounded by a growing number of housing areas for the DOSAAF, the Volunteer Society to Support the Army, Aviation and the Fleet. Aircraft that were normally based here included VIP aircraft and a number of Soviet Air Force helicopters.

A number of wrecked aircraft, including Mi-2s, Yak-18Ts and a Lesunov Li-2 litter the field. When I visited the field for the first time in August of 1991, I climbed over a large fence only to discover that a few hundred feet away was an open gate. MiG-29s and Su-27s from Kubinka Air Force Base performed aerobatic trials over the airfield in preparation of the Aviation Day air show. Paratroops practiced their routine from a DOSAAF An-2 and a number of Polish built Mi-2 Hoplite helicopters were practicing formation flying.

Army personnel were always present but did not seem to care when a Westerner approached and took pictures. So apart from the fact that I was almost over-run by a Yak-18T, the visit had no unusual incidents.

One year later there were a number of changes at Tushino. There were a number of new color schemes applied on the aircraft. The former DOSAAF Mi-2 Hoplites were all absorbed by the National Aero Club of Russia while some cannibalized Mi-2s were being used as a source of spare parts. The An-2s, some of which had previously flown with Aeroflot or DOSAAF, had received new Russian registrations. There was a mixture of old Soviet SSSR (CCCP) registrations on the wings and the new Russian registration applied on the fin and fuselage.

The An-24B; used for VIP transport, received the new Russian fin flash that replaced the Red Star. One of the An-26s also received new Russian markings, but retained the Soviet registration. Tushino had not lost its importance for VIP flights, which were now performed for the Yelzin government.

Three An-32s were flown directly from the manufacturer to Tushino. Although two of them carried Soviet Air Force markings (without tactical numbers), they now belong to private enterprises. Due to the new political and economic situation; the former State Aircraft Factories now sell factory fresh surplus transport aircraft directly to private owners. One of the An-32s served as living quarters for an entire family, with some kids hanging out in the cockpit and other people seeking protection from the sun in the fuselage.

The same aircraft was still at Tushino a year later in August of 1992, however, it looked rather well worn. Yellow 05 still carried the DOSAAF logo under the cockpit in Yellow. The aircraft is unusual in that it carries the Red star national insignia on the wing uppersurfaces.

This former Aeroflot An-2T carries the old Soviet Registration SSSR (CCCP)-70322 on the wing uppersurface, while on the fuselage it has the new number 01217 (although the Russian registration prefix is missing). Thid aircraft, like many of the other An-2s at Tushino, was very weathered.

This former Aeroflot An-2T has the Aeroflot lettering on the fuselage overpainted, but the Soviet fin flash is still in place. The upper wing has the Soviet registration SSSR-98100 and the fuselage has the new registration FLARF-01101.

This White with Blue and Red trim An-2T has the new Russian fin flash, the registration FLASSSR-01100 on the fuselage along with the logos left over from a good will flight to Australia.

Almost every An-2 at Tushino carried a different color schemes and there are also differences in Russia registration prefixes. This former Aeroflot An-2T carried the registration FLARF-02220.

After its final flight this Su-22M-4 Fitter K, Yellow 546, had its East German markings overpainted with a Dark Green paint. Reportedly, this Fitter K will be preserved. (Jens Schymura)

Although an order was issued that all former East German aircraft should be re-painted with a four digit West German registration number, this was not always strictly followed. This Su-22M-4 Fitter K (Serial 26817) Red 757, formerly of the 28th Naval Fighter Regiment still carried its former East German tactical number during April of 1993. Additionally, it still carried the 'Winged Q' maintenance award symbol behind the tactical number. The West German registration number Black 25 42, was intended for this aircraft, but had just not been painted on for some unknown reason. (E. Prell)

A pair of Su-22M-4s stored in the open at Laage-Kronskamp during April of 1993. The aircraft in the background has the West German inventory number Black 25 28 (ex Red 598) with a thin small White outlined, while the Fitter K in the foreground, Black 28 38 (ex Red 734), has unoutlined numbers. Both aircraft once belonged to the 28th Marine Fighter Regiment. (E. Prell)

A line-up of Su-22M-4 Fittter Ks on the apron of Laage-Kronskamp. All aircraft have had the the K-36D ejection seat removed and replaced with ballast to act as a balance weight . Additionally, some of the electronic equipment used on the Fitters was canibalized for use on the MiG-29 Fulcrums retained in West German service. (E. Prell)

This Su-22M-4 Fitter K (Serial 31203), Black 25+33, was being prepared for a ferry flight to Ramstein Air Force Base on 25 March 1991. The Fitter, formerly of the 28th Naval Fighter Regiment, was then handed over to the U.S. Air Force. After being prepared for transport, it was loaded aboard a C-5 Galaxy. A total of four Fitter Ks were turned over to the USAF. (Eckhardt Prell)

Blue 798, the specially painted Su-22M-4 Fitter K on its hardstand at Laage-Kronskamp. The aircraft has had the rear ASO-2V chaff/flare dispenser unit removed, leaving a natural metal strip visible below the fin, while the front ASO-2V chaff/flare dispenser unit remain in place on the aircraft. The covered aircraft in the background are MiG-23 Floggers and Su-22 Fitters. (Jens Schymura)

This An-26T (Serial 14208) once served as Black 373 in the East German Air Force and was used for Electronic Intelligence (ELINT) missions. The Curl was taken into service by the West German Air Force with the registration Black 52+10. (Wolfgang Tamme)

When the 3rd Assault Helicopter Regiment was disbanded at Cottbus on 31 March 1993, this Mi-8TB was repainted in this special "Turtle" color scheme. The Hip had once flown as Black 125 before getting the West German registration, Black 94+62. (Klaus Meissner)

Later, the former Elint Curl Black 52+10 was cannibalized at Dresden in order to supply the An-26SM, Black 52+09, used for navaid calibration flights with a supply of spare parts. (Wolfgang Tamme)

A East German Mi-2 was given this special color scheme for Flying Doctor work; however, it only carried these colors for two weeks before it was repainted in standard camouflage colors. It served with KHG-3 Assault Helicopter Regiment. (Klaus Meissner)

According the lettering on the rear fuselage, this An-2T, Black 75, was demonstrated in the United States during 1991. The aircraft carries, just above the main landing gear leg, a small American flag.

This An-2T, Red 08, belongs to the new Lithuanian Air Force. The aircraft were former Soviet Air Force Colts, taken over and repainted by the Lithuanian. The insignia is the same as that used by the LAF in the period prior to the Second World War. (G. Ramoska)

Two camouflaged DOSAAF An-2s flank a White civil registered An-2. The Colt in the foreground carries a White tactical number on the fuselage side. It is unusual for An-2s to carry any tactical number.

This An-2T, Black 26, carries a Soviet flag fin flash and Red star national markings on the upper wing surface. The aircraft is used by the Podolsk Sewing Machine Works. The lettering "90 Let" means 90 years and "Chaika" or Gull is the trade name of one of their products.

These two former Soviet Air Force An-2 Colt biplane transports were absorbed into the Lithuanian Air Force. Most of the more modern equipment was flown out of Lithuania when the Soviets withdrew from the country, although it is known that several L-39s were also taken over and repainted with Lithuanian markings. (G. Ramoska)

An abandoned An-26 Curl turboprop transport, Red 61, on the grass at Tushino. The tactical number had a thin small Black outline. A Red tactical number usually denotes a Guards Regiment.

The Kremlin style of star national marking is not widely used. The star is outlined with a large White area and thin Red outline. The tactical number, Yellow 01, has no outline.

Tushino is surrounded by high rise buildings that serve as living quarters and offices for the field. The aircraft in the foreground is a factory fresh An-32 with a dome observation window.

An An-24B, Red 01, starts its two AI-24VT turoprop engines with the help of a RU-19A-300 auxiliary power unit that is fitted on the port engine in the rear of the cowling. The aircraft carries an unusual style national marking on the tail.

In the Summer of 1992, this same An-24B, Yellow 01, was repainted with the new White/Blue/Red Russian fin flash. The tactical number was also redone, with Black shadow shading applied to the number.

This overall Natural Metal MiG-17F Fresco C, at the Aeroking KFT storage depot carries fake Soviet Air Force markings. The vehicle in the background is a Soviet-built Kamaz truck.

(Left) This MiG-15bis (Serial 31530981), Red 981, is one of some forty-one aircraft and helicopters stored at the Vecses storage depot near the Budapest international airport.

This MiG-17PF Fresco D, Red 1975, has a fire blackened canopy, indicating that at one time the aircraft was used for crash/rescue and fire fighting training. The S-13 gun camera is missing and the radome was damaged.

(Left) A line-up of MiG-15bis and MiG-17PF fighters at the Vecses storage depot. Only a few of the aircraft were reassembled after being delivered here. The tactical number and national markings were overpainted on the aircraft in the foreground.

A PZL-101 Gawron (Rook) wing is stored beside two Mi-1 helicopter fuselages. In among the other parts scattered around the yard are the nose sections of two MiG-21s.

This MiG-21F-13 Fishbed C, Red 1281, has a damaged tail section and part of the dorsal spine covering is missing.

This new production An-32 carried full Soviet Air Force markings during the Summer of 1992; however, the aircraft was actually owned by a private company and was being used as living quarters.

One of a number of new production An-32s at Tushino. Although these aircraft carried full Soviet Air Force markings and colors. The aircraft has no tactical numbers, indicating that it is not on active military duty.

This privately operated An-32B (SSSR-48075) was repainted with a civil color scheme with the logo of its new owner Air Pavelonik on the fuselage side in Blue. The upper fuselage was in White while the lower half of the fuselage retained the original Soviet Air Force Light Gray color.

This PZL-104, Blue 16, was used by DOSAAF during the Summer of 1991. The aircraft was a Polish design that saw widespread service in the Soviet Union. The An-2 in the background was also built by PZL.

This Su-26 sport aircraft, on the ramp at Tushino, carries a Yellow and Black paint scheme with the Red Soviet star on the fin. The Star has a thin Red outline around the Yellow border.

This Lisunov Li-2 transport (serial 23441605), Yellow 03, was undergoing restoration during the Summer of 1992. The aircraft had the rudder replaced although the elevators are still missing. The Li-2 was a copy of the American Douglas DC-3 (C-47)

A rather weathered and worn Il-14P, Red 01, on the grass at Tushino during the Summer of 1992. Most of the windows in the aircraft were missing and the radome on the upper fuselage was gone.

This Yak-18T has protective covers placed over the engine, cockpit and tail group. These covers are designed to protect aircraft stored in the open against the harsh weather, especially during a Russian Winter.

With the end of the communist era, many Russian civil aircraft received colorful paint schemes. This former DOSAAF Yak-18T undergoing engine maintenance was painted White with Red and Black trim. The registration number was in White against the Red trim on the fin.

An overall White Soviet Air Force Yak-18T, Black 0, runs up its engine on the grass at Tushino. The aircraft tactical number is repeated in White on the underside of the Red outer wing panel. The anti-glare panel on the nose is in Blue and the stripes on the fuselage and tail are Red

Yellow 03 is a Soviet Air Force Mi-2 Hoplite. The aircraft is Olive Green over Light Blue. The aircraft was being prepared for the Aviation Day air show held at Tushino during the Summer of 1991. The Hoplite was built in Poland by the PZL company.

This stored Soviet Air Force Mi-2 Hiplite has a protective cover over the entire forward fuselage. The main rotors have been removed while the tail rotor remains in place. It is believed that this Hoplite was serving as a source of spare parts to maintain others on the field.

An Olive Green over Light Blue Mi-2 Hoplite covered and secured on a hardstand at Tushino during August 1991. Most of these aircraft were later transferred to private owners. Hoplites were produced by PZL at Swidnik, Poland; however, most were exported to the Soviet Union.

This Mi-2 Hoplite, Yellow 23, participated in the Helicopter Championship held in France. The Soviet team was sponsored by the French ANIRAL-UTEC company and ever after the championships were over, the Hoplite continued to carry the special paint scheme it used for the event.

In the Summer of 1990, all the Mi-2s that took part in the Helicopter Championships in France were put into storage at Tushino. Yellow 06 was one of these although the cover over the forward fuselage carries the number of a different Hoplite, Red 04.

Two abandoned Mi-2s on the grass at Tushino during the Summer of 1991. Both aircraft have their main rotor removed and have the rotor head sealed in a protective cover. The forward fuselage also has a protective cover in place over the cockpit glass. The Soviet star insignia on the aircraft in the foreground is very weathered.

This former DOSAAF Mi-2 Hoplite was obtained by the Russian National Aero Club at Tushino and given the registration FLA-07. Athough now a civil aircraft, the basic Soviet Air Force color scheme was retained, except for the White/Blue/Red markings on the engine cover. The aircraft carries an external fuel tank on the fuselage pylon.

A Mi-2, FLA-01, of the National Aero Club of Russia on the ramp at Tushino during the Summer of 1992. The old wooden hangar in the background is now used as a warehouse and did not house aircraft or helicopters. The stripes on the engine housing were (top to bottom) White/Blue/Red while the tail rotor was Black with Red/White/Red tips. The engine exhausts had Red protective covers installed and the aircraft was configured with an external fuel tank.

This Soviet Air Force Mi-8T, Yellow 01, carries a three tone camouflage of Light Green, Olive Drab and Earth Brown over Light Blue. This particular Hip C was also equipped with two 500 liter (132 gallon) auxiliary fuel tanks in the fuselage.

This Mi-8T Hip, Yellow 79, parked on the grass at Tushino in August of 1991 carried a camouflage pattern of Light Gray and Olive Green. Mi-8s in the Soviet Air Force carried a wide variety of camouflage patterns and colors. The tail rotor was Gray with Red tips.

An Olive Green and Light Gray camouflaged Mi-8T Hip C, Yellow 79, is refueled on a hardstand at Tushino. The fuel capacity of the Mi-8 Hip C is 1,870 liters (494 gallons) and refueling is usually done with the engine running and the main rotor engaged at idle.

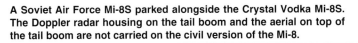

This private, overall White with Blue trim, Mi-8S SSSR-13337 (CCCP-13337) is operated by the Crystal Vodka factory. Interestingly, the lettering is in English not Cyrillic. The main and tail rotor blades, rotor head and cockpit all have protective covers in place, indicating that this Mi-8 has not been flown for a long time.

A number of Soviet Air Force Hip helicopters were still based at Tushino during the Summer of 1992. The Hip in the foreground is a Mi-8S, carrying a two tone Green tone camouflage, while the Hip in the background is a Mi-8T with a three tone camouflage, consisting of Light Green, Olive Drab and Earth Brown.

A Soviet Air Force Mi-8S parked alongside the Crystal Vodka Mi-8S. The Doppler radar housing on the tail boom and the aerial on top of the tail boom are not carried on the civil version of the Mi-8.

This Mi-8T Hip, Red 07, is undergoing an engine overhaul, performed in the open at Tushino in the Summer of 1991. All the engine access hatches are open giving a good view of the TV-2-117 power plant. The insides of the access panels are painted Light Blue, additionally, the main engine access panels also serve as work stands, being capable of supporting the weight of a maintenance man.

Strangers In A Strange Land

The F-5A Freedom Fighter and F-5E Tiger II were developed by the Northrop Company for export customers looking for a cheap and efficient fighter aircraft and both enjoyed a tremendous export success. That the type would find its way to the Soviet Union, Czechoslovakia and Poland was hardly the intention of the manufacturer and the United States government.

Operation SKOSHI TIGER, was an evaluation of the F-5A under tropical conditions in Southeast Asia, since it was foreseen that the type would be used to re-equip the South Vietnamese Air Force.

On 23 October 1965 twelve F-5As of the 4503rd Tactical Fighter Squadron arrived at Bien Hoa Air Base in Vietnam. Within five hours after their arrival, they were used for operational missions against the NVA (North Vietnamese Army). The F-5A achieved the highest operational readiness rate and lowest maintenance man hours per flight hour of any fighter in Vietnam. On 17 April 1967, seventeen F-5C and two F-5B were transferred to the 522nd Fighter Squadron of South Vietnamese Air Force at Tan Son Nhut Air Base.

Before the fall of Saigon and the victory of the Communists in Vietnam, there were some 153 F-5A, F-5B, F-5E and RF-5As delivered to South Vietnam. Some were supplied from the stocks of the Air Forces of Iran, South Korea and Taiwan.

In 1974, a year before the cease fire, there were four South Vietnamese Squadrons equipped with Freedom Fighters and a further three with the F-5E. A lack of sufficient spare parts and sometimes insufficient and unqualified maintenance personnel drastically reduced the combat-readiness of the type.

On 28 February 1975, the NVA launched its last large scale assault, the Great Spring Offensive, in South Vietnam. The important harbor city of Da Nang was overrun and this signaled the end of the regime of President Nguyen Van Thieu. At this time, the South Vietnamese Air Force had 972 operational aircraft in its inventory, including 92 A-37 Dragonflys and 93 F-5s.

On 30 April 1975, the NVA marched into Saigon, which they later renamed Ho Chi Minh City in honor of the leader of the Communist movement in Vietnam. The Communist victory reunited both Vietnams and grounded the fourth largest Air Force in the world.

About 200 South Vietnamese aircraft escaped out of the country, 132 of them sought refuge at U Tapao Air Base in neighboring Thailand,

The ex-Vietnamese F-5E is parked at Okecie airport next to a SBLim-2, Red 002, that was used for various trials, including ejection seat tests. Both aircraft belong to the Instytut Lotnictwa (Flight Institute). The F-5E had been kept under tight security until 1990. (Wojciech Luczak)

including twenty-two F-5Es and a single RF-5A, some of the Northrops were subsequently shipped back to Guam and later to the United States aboard the USS MIDWAY.

The major portion of the VNAF; however, remained in-country. There were about 1,109 aircraft and helicopters which fell into the hands of the Communists. According American intelligence reports, there were sixty F-5As, twenty-seven F-5Es, ninety-five A-37s, twenty-six A-1s, thirty-eight C-47s, fourteen C-130s and thirty-three C-7As. Some of these found their way into the North Vietnamese Air Force inventory.

On 30 May 1975, two new Regiments within the Vietnamese People's Air Force were activated, the 935th Regiment with the F-5s and the 937th Regiment with the A-37s. Most of the former South Vietnamese aircraft retained their original American camouflage and maintenance instructions, but all were repainted with the national insignia of the Vietnamese People's Air Force.

The A-37s and F-5s saw action during the Vietnamese invasion of Cambodia which began in December 1975. A lack of spare parts forced the withdrawal the A-37s from use and by the early 1990s only a few F-5Es remained in service.

The captured material was also of great interest for the Soviet Union, a close ally of the Hanoi Regime. The United States had wisely withdrawn all the intelligence sensitive material from Vietnam after the cease fire of 27 January 1973, but the investigation of some of the captured aircraft was nevertheless of interest for the Soviet Union in order to obtain data on construction techniques used on American aircraft.

At least two F-5E Tiger IIs were shipped to the Soviet Union shortly after the Communist victory. In addition, the Hanoi government offered

The Northrop fighter was jacked up during the evaluation by the PZL company in their hangar at Okecie. A lot of the internal equipment was removed for closer examination by various experts in the Polish aviation industry. (Wojciech Luczak)

This ex-South Vietnamese Air Force (VNAF) F-5E (73-00852) is stored in the open at Okecie, Warsaw's international airport near the PZL hangar where it has been stored for years during the communist era. All its former Vietnamese markings (both VNAF and North Vietnamese) were overpainted. (Wojciech Luczak)

This F-5E (73-00878) Tiger II was delivered to the Czechs at Kbely airfield during 1981. Like the F-5 that went to Poland, this F-5E was ex-VNAF and North Vietnamese Air Force. The aircraft had all of the Vietnamese and tactical markings overpainted with Medium Green and Dark Green paint. (Otakar Saffek)

The Czech F-5E parked in front of the hangar where the aircraft had been stored for years under great security precautions. The secret that a F-5E was in Czechoslovakia was revealed to the public during December of 1989. (Otakar Saffek)

captured material to other members of the Eastern Bloc. Most of the actual evaluation work on the captured aircraft was made at Zhukovsky and involved a number of institutions, such as the Central Aero and Hydrodynamics Institute (TSAGI), the Central Aero-Engine institute (TSIAM) and the All-Union Institute for Aviation Materials (VIAM). The various Design Bureaus such as MiG, Sukhoi and Yakovlev also benefited in these investigations.

Some of the captured material was also delivered from Vietnam to Poland and Czechoslovakia. The shipments to both countries being done under very strict security measures. In September of 1977, two containers from Vietnam arrived aboard a merchant ship in the Polish harbor at Gdynia. One container contained an A-37B Dragonfly and another held a F-5E Tiger II (73-00852), the latter previously flew with the 23rd Tactical Fighter Wing and had been captured at Tan Sop Nhut airfield in April of 1975.

The dark patch on the tail of the Czech F-5E shows where the South Vietnamese squadron code on the stabilizer was overpainted. The rear covering of the General Electric J-85-GE-21 power plant had been replaced from another aircraft with a different camouflage pattern. The aircraft still carried full American maintenance inscriptions. (Otakar Saffek)

The F-5E was shipped to Czechoslovakia from Vietnam in two containers. In addition to the basic aircraft, three 275 gallon external fuel tanks and several AIM-9 Sidewinder missiles were also supplied. The wing tip AIM-9 missile launcher is not complete on the aircraft that is on display. (Otakar Saffek)

A group of military personnel disassembled both jets, working without any instructions or technical data from the Vietnamese. The aircraft were then loaded onto railway cars, camouflaged and sent to Warsaw. Here they were turned over to the military experts from the Technical Institute of the Polish Air Force.

Both jets were re-assembled and all systems ground tested including engines and guns. In 1977 air tests were considered, however, no one in authority wanted to issue the permits to conduct the flights. Finally, in December of 1977 at the Warsaw-Bemowo air base, which was closed to the public, a ground taxi demonstration was organized for military authorities, technical military personnel and aviation scientists. Everything was kept very confidential.

Reportedly the reason for the delivery of the F-5E was to investigate the possibility to convert the aircraft to carry two Soviet manufactured Nudelman Richter NR-23 23MM cannon capable of firing 850 rounds per minute. The entire project was later cancelled. There were no evaluations flights in Poland, so the aircraft did not carry Polish military insignia.

The A-37B Dragonfly was presented to the Instytut Lotnictwa on 5 May 1981 with the Tiger II following on 14 February 1983. At that time, the Instytut Lotnictwa, which is not a military organization was working on the W-300 project, which developed into the I-22 Iryda jet trainer.

It was decided that everybody working on the W-300 project was to be given an insight to western manufacturing and design technology. So

The Polish F-5E was closely investigated by the Polish aviation industry in order to gain some insight into American construction techniques and hopefully to transfer some of this technology into the I-22 trainer project. These two I-22 prototypes are on the ramp at Okecie airfield carrying temporary civil registrations. In the event, very little, if any F-5 technology went into the I-22. (Wojciech Luczak)

during the I-22 design phase practically every Northrop and Cessna system was closely examined once again, this time to give them an insight on techniques that might assist with work on the I-22. The Tiger II's ejection seat was of particular interest, although in the end nothing from either jet was copied for the I-22 project.

The F-5E, surrounded by a high yellow plastic barricade, was guarded by an Army sentry in a large hangar of the PZL Company at Okecie. Although the real owner on the Tiger II was the Instytut Lotnictwa, the aircraft was stored in the PZL Company hangar due to space problems. A very limited number of persons knew of the existence of the two American built aircraft in Poland.

With the end of Communist rule in Poland, the F-5E was re-assembled and revealed for the first time to the public in late 1990. It is now stored in the open at Warsaw's international airport at Okecie.

In 1981, a single F-5E (73-00878) was shipped by sea to Czechoslovakia, together with two AIM-9 Sidewinder missiles and several pieces of ground equipment, in two L-39 Albatros shipping containers.

Similar to the Polish experience, the Vietnamese had sent no technical documents or manuals, so test flights with the Tiger II were never even considered. The aircraft was sent to Kbely airfield, home of the Flight Test and Evaluation Center of the Czech Air Force on the outskirts of Prague. There the aircraft was closely studied by VZS technicians. The plane was carefully dismantled and analyzed. Besides the experts of the Flight and Evaluation Center (VZS), technicians from the Aero factory at Vodochody also joined the evaluation team.

Aero had hoped that careful analyses of the design and manufacturing

The Czech Aero Company at Vodochody hoped to transfer some of the F-5 technology to gain some improvements in its own designs, such as the L-39 Albatros, which had also been exported to Vietnam. (Jens Schymura)

techniques of the F-5 could help improve the Aero L-39 Albatros jet trainer, which was the standard trainer for the Warsaw Pact nations and had been exported to a number of other countries, including Vietnam. Eventually, very little of the F-5's technology could be actually transferred to Albatros production at Vodochody.

Eventually, the F-5E was partially re-assembled and stored in one of the hangars at the Air and Cosmos Museum at Khely.

Not all Western aircraft which found their way East of the Iron Curtain were captured. This Vertol H-21 helicopter (N74056) was a gift of the United States of America to the Soviet Union. It now rests in the Museum at Monino.

Germany

On 3 October 1990, East and West Germany were reunited. From a historical point of view it was a reunificition, but from the political, commercial and military point of view it was an occupation of the former German Democratic Republic by West Germany, since all important posts came under control of the Federal Republic of Germany. On this fateful date, the former East Germany also became a member of NATO.

Ironically the end of East Germany did not start within the country itself, but some one thousand miles away, on the Hungarian/Austrian border. When Hungary tore down the Iron Curtain on 2 May 1989, this allowed East German citizens to travel to the West. The steady flow of hundreds of skilled workers to West Germany severely affected the East German economy. Riots broke out and the communist party was helpless to halt the outward flow of people. On 9 November 1989, the Berlin Wall fell.

The entire arsenal, worth some sixty million U.S. dollars, of the former *Nationale Volksarmee* (East German Army) had been absorbed into the *Bundeswehr* (West German Army), including some 440 aircraft and 218 helicopters of the *Luftstreitkraefte* (East German Air Force). But for the new owner this was an unwanted heritage from the communist era rather than a valuable addition to its own arsenal.

The material, mainly of Soviet design, could not be easily absorbed into the West German inventory. With the exception of the MiG-29 Fulcrum, all other combat aircraft were not into active status by the *Bundesluftwaffe* and as a result all combat units; with the exception of the 3rd Fighter Regiment (flying the Fulcrum) were disbanded and their aircraft put into storage. The economic result of this decision on the former German Democratic Republic was devastating as highly qualified pilots and ground personnel lost their jobs. Due to the severe economic difficulties in the former East Germany, it was and is, extremely difficult for them to find adequate work.

The end for the DDR (*Deutsche Demokratische Republik*/German Democratic Republic) came for many, including most of the prominent West European politicians, unexpectedly soon. When it became apparent that the country would soon disappear from the maps of Europe, East Germany's Ministry of Defense, lead by Rainer Eppelmann, went to great efforts to sell as much as possible of its arms to foreign customers through official and unofficial channels. A number of East German offi-

This MiG-2 F-13, Red 716, served with the advanced training regiment FAG-15 at Rothenburg before it was struck of charge on 30 November 1978 and taken to Marxwalde Air Base to serve as a decoy. After reunification, the East German national markings were overpainted. (Simon Watson)

cers, arms dealers and politicians were involved in these affairs and arms transactions.

One of the many various negotiations for the sale of East German material involved India, which was interested in obtaining some 300 T-55 and T-72 tanks as well as spare parts for MiG-21 Fishbeds. Other items had been offered to Algeria, Zambia, Uganda, Iraq and Yemen. In the Summer of 1990, arms dealers in East Germany where about to deliver a number of tanks to Iraq, but this transaction was halted by customs.

On 28 September 1990, a few days before re-unification, C.I.C. International Ltd. of New York signed a contract for the delivery of some forty MiG-21s, forty MiG-23s, twenty-five Su-22M-4 Fitter Ks, plus 1,200 T-55 and 200 T-72 tanks for a subsequent resale in various other countries, including Pakistan. Further negotiations with West Germany followed, but, in the event, the goods were never transferred to C.I.C. International Ltd.

Many of the deals could not be executed before re-unification, since the West German government closely monitored these activities, when it became clear that East Germany was starting a bargain sell out of its arsenals. Arms, valuing about 500 Million U.S. Dollars had already been sold and goods worth another 80 Million U.S. Dollars had been exported to Hungary and another 130 Million Dollars worth had been sent to Poland.

Some East German MiG-21F-13 Fishbed Cs were used as decoys on East German Air Bases. Since these aircraft already had been struck of charge before the reunification, they were never given West German four digit registration numbers and taken into the West German inventory system. (Simon Watson)

This MiG-21M (Serial 0410, Red 560) once served with the 9th Fighter Regiment, Heinrich Rau, before it was withdrawn from service on 10 January 1974 and taken to the Officer's Academy at Kamenz. After unification, the East German national markings were overpainted. (Wolfgang Tamme)

This MiG-21M (Serial 1111, ex-Red 611) once served with the tactical reconnaissance squadron (TAFS-47) at Preschen. Since this Fishbed was not retained for flight tests, it was painted with the four digit black registration number, 22 89, and given a Federal Republic fin flash instead of full West German markings. (Jens Schymura)

Stored behind barbed wire at Drewitz Air Base, some 140 Fishbeds awaited their final fate. By late 1994, all of these former East German MiG-21s will be scraped at Dresden. On the left is Black 22 50, which once flew as Red 432, with the 1st Fighter Regiment, while the Mongol on the right, Black 23 75 (formerly Black 253) was part of the 2nd Fighter Regiment. (Jens Schymura)

The West German Government was very strict in exporting former East German material to non-NATO countries and eventually decided it would be politically less trouble to scrap the material in Germany rather to sell it abroad. All aircraft and helicopters which were in the inventory of the *Luftstreitkraefte* at the time of re-unification received a four digit Black inventory number. The three digit tactical number, standard on the East German aircraft, Red for combat and Black for all other types, had to be overpainted, as did the East German national markings. On the tail fin a small Black/Red/Yellow fin flash, the national insignia of the Federal Republic of Germany was added on all aircraft and helicopters.

There was, at the beginning, some confusion with the painting orders issued by the *Bundesluftwaffe*, and some aircraft received full West German markings. Most aircraft received the four digit code in Black on the nose, but on some aircraft there was also a dash added between the 2nd and the 3rd digit.

Only the aircraft which were intended for evaluation flights or were being absorbed into the *Bundesluftwaffe* (West German Air Force) received full Air Force markings. For some special occasions, such as photographic sessions, the Iron Cross was applied to former East German aircraft. For those aircraft which were to be stored or scrapped, these markings were short lived and were soon overpainted. Aircraft being flown to the storage/destruction sites at Laage-Kronskamp and Drewitz were flown without full West German Air Force markings, carrying only the fin flash and four digit code.

In addition to the *Bundesluftwaffe*, the Royal Air Force and USAF were eager to investigate modern equipment of Soviet manufacture. A

Some of the stored aircraft at Drewitz Air Base are well covered with canvas covers, such as this MiG-21UM, but most have no protection from the weather. (Jens Schymura)

A line-up of some of the covered MiG-21 Fishbeds parked behind barbed wire at Drewitz Air Base near the Polish border. The aircraft in the center is a MiG-21MF (Serial 6213, Black 23 36) which once served with the 1st Fighter Regiment as Red 683. (Marcus Fulber)

This MiG-23MF (Serial 0390213299) was formerly assigned to the 9th Fighter Regiment, Heinrich Rau, during August of 1978 as Red 577. After re-unification it was flown to Laage-Kronskamp Air Base for storage with the West German registration Black 20-02. (Marcus Fulber)

request issued by the American Defense Department was turned over to the West German government, asking for a single MiG-29 Fulcrum, two Su-22M-4 Fitter Ks and five MiG-23ML Floggers. In March of 1991 the newly established 5th Air Division of the West German Air Force at Strausberg received orders that two Su-22M-4s and five MiG-23MLs, all stored at Laage-Kronskamp be prepared for a ferry flight to Ramstein Air Force Base. Since all of these aircraft had been stored for a long period in a non-operational status, they were all carefully checked by maintenance personnel.

The pilots selected to ferry the two Su-22M-4s were briefed and given a check out flight in a two seat Su-22UM-3K, followed by a check out in the single seat Fitter K. Although both the 28th Naval Fighter Regiment and the 77th Fighter Bomber Regiment were both deactivated at this

This MiG-23MF Flogger G (Serial 0390213100) once flew as Red 585 with the 2nd Squadron of the 9th Fighter Regiment. Although it was never selected for flight evaluation, it carried full German Air Force markings for a short period of time. (Marcus Fulber)

Stored at Laage-Kronskamp, this MiG-23ML (Serial 0390324636, ex-Red 340) now carries the West German registration Black 20 17. The insignia of its former operator, the 9th Fighter Regiment remains on the fin. (Jens Schymura)

This MiG-23ML Flogger G (Serial 0390324033) Black 20 32, was being readied for a ferry flight from Laage-Kronskamp to Ramstein AFB on 27 March 1991. At Ramstein the former Red 567 was handed over to the USAF and flown to the United States aboard a C-5 Galaxy. (Eckhardt Prell)

This MiG-23UM (Serial Number A1037901, Black 104) formerly of the 37th Fighter Bomber Regiment Klement Gottwald was flown to Laage-Kronskamp for storage with the West German registration number Black 20 62. The unit badge of the 37th Fighter Bomber Regiment was still on the air intake duct. (Jens Schymura)

This Su-22M-4 (Serial 255509, Red 362) was among the first batch of six Fitter Ks which arrived in East Germany on 8 December 1984. These aircraft had been ferried into Germany aboard An-22 and Il-76 transports. Later the aircraft was stored at Laage-Kronskamp Air Base and given the West German registration number, Black 25 02. (Eckhardt Prell)

A line-up of Su-22M-4 Fitter Ks at Laage-Kronskamp during the Summer of 1992. All had been covered with White canvas covers with the former East German tactical number sprayed in Black on the cover. The letter M indicates the aircraft is a single seat Fitter K. (Jens Schymura)

This MiG-23BN (Serial 0393211085) once served as Red 689 with the 37th Fighter Bomber Regiment, Klement Gottwald at Drewitz. After reunification, it received the West German registration number Black 20 38 and had a small Federal Germany fin flash painted on the fin. (Wolfgang Tamme)

time, several pilots were recalled to active duty for the flight.

The pilots of the 9th Fighter Regiment which was equipped with the MiG-23MF and MiG-23ML had all been discharged from the Air Force and as a result, pilots from the 37th Fighter Bomber Regiment, once equipped with the MiG-23BN ferried the five Flogger Gs. Since none of the 37th Fighter Bomber regiment pilots had ever flown the fighter version, several check out flights were conducted at Laage-Kronskamp before the actual mission.

On 25 March 1993, *Hauptmann* (Captain) Hansi Lange and *Kapitaenleutnant* (1st Lieutenant) Ulli Schneider were briefed to ferry the two Su-22M-4s, 25+25 (ex Red 380) and 25+33 (ex Red 724). Both aircraft carried full West German markings for the flight. Shortly after takeoff the Fitters were joined by two F-4 Phantoms which acted as escort. This was necessary since the Fitter Ks did not carry the proper IFF transponders.

Near Frankfurt/Main the four ship formation was joined by two USAF F-16s. The landing at Ramstein AFB was without incident and immediately after landing the two Su-22M-4s were towed into highly guarded shelters.

Few hours prior the arrival of the two Fitter Ks at Ramstein, all technical equipment, ground support equipment, SFS radar jamming pods, SPPU-22 cannon pods and KKR reconnaissance pods were also transferred aboard an An-26 Curl of *Lufttransportgeschwader* 65 (Air Transport Regiment 65). At that time, no Soviet air-to-air missiles were transferred to the USAF.

On 27 and 28 March 1991, the five MiG-23MLs were also transferred from Laage-Kronskamp to Ramstein using a similar procedure. The five

A pair of Fitters stored at the apron of Laage-Kronskamp. On the left is a Su-22UM-3K trainer (Serial 69809, ex-Black 113) coded Black 25 47, while the aircraft on the right is a Su-22M-4 Fitter K (Serial 31204, ex-Red 728) coded Black 25 36 . The unit badge usually found at the base of the fin on the Fitter K was overpainted with Red paint. (Jens Schymura)

Besides aircraft, a large number of external fuel tanks, weapon racks, rocket pods and ammunition had to be disposed of. The tanks are PTB-1150 drop tanks for use on the Fitter. The rocket pods next to them are thirty-two shot UB-32M pods for the S-5 rockets while the pods at the far right are B-8M1 pods for the S-8 rocket. (Eckhardt Frell)

MiG-23ML were: 25-15 (ex Red 338), 20-16 (ex Red 339), 20-28 (ex Red 551), 20-32 (ex Red 567) and 20-36 (ex Red 606). In contrast to the Su-22M-4s, the Floggers did not carry full West German markings.

The single MiG-29 Fulcrum A, 29+06 (ex Red 661), that had been requested by the USAF arrived directly from 3rd Fighter Regiment home base Preschen.

Under strict security measures, the aircraft were dismantled and ferried to the U.S aboard an USAF C-5 Galaxy.

In addition, there were a number of aircraft and helicopters allocated to various military schools and training centers. Others, especially MiG-21F-13s were used as decoys on various air force bases. All these did not receive registration numbers. On most; however, the East German national markings were overpainted, while the tactical number was retained.

Later, it was decided to concentrate all former East German Air Force combat aircraft intended for storage/scrap on three major air bases. Most MiG-21s were sent to Drewitz, which also housed a number of MiG-23BNs. Three MiG-23UM had been flown to Laage-Kronskamp near Rostock for storage along with the other remaining MiG-23s and Su-22M-4s. A number of MiG-21s and fifty-two L-39s are stored at Rothenburg Air Base, near Dresden. A number of L-39 are housed in a hangar, while most are parked in the open, protected by canvas covers.

At Laage-Kronskamp Air Base, the most modern of all former East

All Czech-built Aero L-39ZOs are stored at Rothenburg. This L-39ZO (Serial 731006) with the West German registration number, Black 28 06, once flew as Black 144, with Training Regiment FAG 25 Leander Ratz. (Jens Schymura)

Some of the Aero L-39 fleet stored at Rothenburg Air Base is parked outside of the hangars and protected by canvas covers. All L-39 and MiG-21 training aircraft formerly assigned to the two advanced training units, FAG 15 and FAG 25, went to Rothenburg. Some of the L-39s were sold to Hungary. This is a L-39V target tow, identified by its White and Yellow color scheme. (Marcus Fulber)

This rather derelict Yak-11 once belonged the Ist Fighter Regiment and was left behind at Cottbus Air base when the unit moved to Holzdorf Air Base during November of 1982. There were 99 Yak-11s in the inventory of the East German Air Force and some were used to shoot down West German ballons delivering propaganda leaflets over East Germany. (Hans Schreiber)

This Mi-8TB (Serial 10527, ex-Black 911) was struck off charge after an accident on 6 April 1976 and had been taken to the Officer's Academy at Kamenz. After re-unification, the East German national markings were overpainted and the aircraft was otherwise unchanged. (Wolfgang Tamme)

This MiG-21UM (Serial 07695168) once flew with the tactical reconnaissance squadron TAFS-87 from Drewitz as Black 213, before it became Black 23+85 in West Germany. The aircraft carries full West German markings, even though it was never used by the Bundeslaftwaffe. It was the first East German aircraft to be scrapped at Dresden. (Wolfgang Tamme)

German Air Bases, there are seven MiG-23MF Flogger Cs, twenty-two MiG-23ML Flogger Gs, eight MiG-23UM Flogger Bs, forty-two Su-22M-4s and seven Su-22UM-3Ks. A number of these are hangared in

For a week, technicians of the Elbe Flugzeugwerke GmbH stripped down the MiG-23UM, until all that remained was the skeleton of the fuselage. This aircraft was finally destroyed on 22 September 1992. (Andreas Schutz)

The MiG-21UM, Black 23+85 was stripped down of all internal equipment by the Elbe Flugzeugwerke GmbH at Dresden-Klotzsche. The private company is responsible for the scrapping of some 142 MiG-21s. The project was expected to take several years. (Andreas Schutz)

pairs in the hardened shelters on the base, but most are stored in the open.

In July of 1992, the German government announced that the destruction of ll,000 former East German artillery pieces, tanks and combat aircraft would commence on 3 August, under the Conventional Forces in Europe agreement. As a result, some 140 MiG-21 Fishbeds were scrapped at Dresden. The total cost of of this effort is estimated to be some 120 Million U.S. Dollars. Interestingly, some of the MiG-21bis Fishbed L/Ns being scrapped are of a newer manufacturing date than the F-4 Phantom II and Alpha Jets currently in service with the West German Air Force.

The goal of the West German government is that the total number of combat aircraft in the inventory of the *Bundesluftwaffe* should be no higher than 500 aircraft by late 1995. This means that besides the MiG-21s, most of the MiG-23s and Su-22s stored at Laage-Kronskamp would also be scrapped, along with a number of aging F-4s and Alpha Jets.

The standard scrap procedure is as follows: the MiG-21 is dismantled into major components at nearby Drewitz Air Base, then taken by truck to Dresden-Klotzsche. The MiGs arrive at a rate of between six to eight per week. After arrival at Dresden, technicians strip the aircraft of usable parts, which will be separately recycled at other locations. The GSh-23L cannons are destroyed by bending the barrels.

The stripped fuselage is then cut down with cutting torches. The process takes about a week and involves about five workers. Recycling the airframe is handled by about thirty employees, most of them former engineers and it is expected that the project will last some two years. The first MiG-21 was destroyed with a cutting torch on 22 September 1992. This ceremony was also attended by Air Force General Eberhard Mende and other high ranking officers. The first aircraft through the process was a MiG-21UM (07695168, ex-Black 213) The destruction of a single MiG-21 Fishbed costs about 33,000 U.S. Dollars.

The twelve An-26Ts, which had been allocated after reunification to *Lufttransportgeschwader* 63, were retained only briefly. In December of 1992 the Curl was retired from active service and most of the An-26Ts were flown to Diepholz, where they were offered for sale in January of 1993. Eight were purchased by the Aeroflot for supply missions to their Arctic stations. On 10 May 1993, the last two An-26T departed from Diepholz to its new home base at Petshora in the Russian Republic of Komi.

A single An-26SM (Serial 11402, ex-Black 52+09) was refurbished in January of 1993 and served as navaid calibration aircraft, while a further An-26 (Serial 14208, ex-Black 52+10) was retained for use as a spare part supplier for the single An-26SM. The remaining Curls were donated to the German Air Force Museum at Appen and the German Museum at Schleissheim.

Dietmar Zumpe, who repaired and maintained MiG-21s for fifteen years, cuts the nose off the fuselage of the first MiG-21UM Black 23+85 to be destroyed at Dresden-Klotzsche. It only took him some three minutes to complete the job. (Andreas Schutz)

A MiG-21M jacked up on dollys where it will be dismantled and stripped down of all its equpiment. Two of the former East German An-26Ts that were taken into service by the West German Bundesluftwaffe are in the backgrouned. (Andreas Schutz)

This MiG-21M (Serial 3205, Black 22 49) once served as Red 431 with the 2nd Fighter Regiment, Juri Gagarin. It rests on jacks in front of the hangars which had been built in the 1950s to build Il-14s under license. The tail fin had been cut from the fuselage with a cutting torch. (Andreas Schutz)

The Remains of Communist Air Power in Hungary

When the Warsaw Pact ceased to exist on 1 April 1991, a completely new political and military situation was created in Eastern Europe.

Due to severe budget cuts, a large bomber of older combat aircraft could no longer be kept operational and were quickly retired and taken to storage depots, transferred to museums, or sold for hard currency to warbird collectors in the West.

Hungary was no exception. Even after the bloody suppression of the population after Imre Nagy's uprising against the Soviet's in October of 1956, the Hungarian's succeeded in maintaining relatively close ties to Western countries. Of all the former Communist countries, Hungary took a leading role towards democracy. Hungarian frontier guards tore down the barbed wire and the wall between their country and neutral Austria in the Autumn of 1989, the first fateful cut in the Iron Curtain!

This decision had fatal results for the German Democratic Republic. From that day onward, thousands of East Germans escaped via Czechoslovakia through Hungary to the West. In most cases, the Germans were not hindered by Hungarian frontier guards. For the East German government this was a disaster and it later led to the fall of the Honecker regime and the fall of the Berlin Wall on 9 November 1989.

During the cold war period it was common that retired fighters and other aircraft were presented as gifts to amusement parks, kindergar-

Some of the MiG-15bis, MiG-15UTI and MiG-17PFs in storage at Vecses, Hungary. Some of the aircraft were reassembled after arrival in the storage depot, while others were in worse condition and were not reassembled. The missile is a SA-2 (SAM-2) Guideline surface-to-air missile of the type widely used in Vietnam.

A cannibalized MiG-15bis, Red 1981, rests in the grass at Vecses. Most of the aircraft's access panels and the rear canopy are missing. The inscription 'W.A.S.P.' on the rear fuselage refers to a popular heavy metal band. This kind of music is very popular in Hungary.

dens, technical schools and other locations. With the end of the communist era, these aircraft lost their importance. Since the bloody 1956 uprising, Hungarian's have been hyper-suspicious of anything with the Red star. Therefore it can be of little surprise that the people wanted to remove the unwanted heritage of the Communist era and the Soviet occupation. As a direct result, the Hungarian Air Force re-introduced their pre-war national markings, applying this marking to combat aircraft in early 1991.

The Hungarian attitude was completely understandable; however, in their rush to rid the country of the Red star, they were also destroying a part of their history. In 1989, very few people considered this fact, but among the few that did were the employees of the Aeroking KFT company in Budapest.

This company quickly begun to remove military and aircraft exhibits

This MiG-15bis (Serial 31530981, Red 981) was one of a few MiG-15s that retained their original three digit tactical numbers that were used while the aircraft was in operational service with the Hungarian Air Force. Most of the aircraft had been repainted at some point with a four digit number.

from all over Hungary, along with aircraft from technical museums and military schools. These were stored, in order to protect them from destruction.

Aeroking KFT succeeded in acquiring a storage depot at Vecses, very close to the International Airport of Budapest-Ferihegy 2. The storage depot was part of a metal and alloy recycling dump which had been established in the same area. The entire depot is surrounded by a fence and guarded by some friendly dogs.

In August of 1990, the first seven dismantled aircraft and a single Mi-1 helicopter arrived at Vecses. In March of 1991, a Polish built PZL-101 Gawron (Rook) and three An-2Ms were transferred from the Pestvideki Gepgyar Overhaul Depot to Vecses. The 41st and thus far last aircraft was taken to the depot on 9 July 1992.

The aircraft are in various condition, some were nearly intact and were reassembled after their arrival at Vecses. Some show signs of extensive damage and have not been re-assembled. Nothing has been done to protect the depot from the weather, which has caused some problems. In addition to the aircraft, a large amount of spare parts were transported to the depot, including two ASh-62IR engines from a Li-2 transport.

Space restrictions forced Aeroking KFT to store a number of MiG-15bis fighters in a second depot within the same area. These aircraft are damaged beyond economical repair and will be cannibalized for spare parts. Since no hangars are available, all the aircraft had to be stored in the open. It is hoped that some of the aircraft can be fully restored and placed in museums.

Aeroking KFT also wants to export or exchange some of the aircraft at Vecses. Negotiations are underway to export a MiG-15UTI and a MiG-21F-13 to England. With the start of the civil war in the former Yugoslavia, plans were cancelled to exchange a MiG-15bis for an F-84 Thunderjet.

A MiG-15bis, coded Red 1977, rests on a mountain of aircraft parts. There are fuselage parts as well the fabric covered rotor blades of an Mi-1 visible in the stack. The national insignia is badly weathered but still visible. Hungary was one of the few Warsaw Pact countries to carry the insignia on both the fuselage and fin.

This overall White MiG-15bis, Red 069, is stored on a separate storage depot half a mile away from the main storage depot. The original canopy glass has been replaced by alloy sheets and the barrel of the N-37 cannon was painted Red.

57

Late in their service lives, Hungarian Air Force MiG-15bis fighters were used in the ground attack role. For this mission they were camouflaged with Dark Green and Earth Brown uppersurfaces over Light Blue undersurfaces. The canopy glass has been broken and the wings, horizontal tail surfaces and other items are on the ground next to the Fagot.

Most of the inventory at Vecses once flew with the Hungarian Air Force, but there is also a Yak-28R in the collection. This aircraft once served with the Soviet Recce-Regiment based at Debrecen. Also part of the collection is a V-750 Dvina, better known in the West as SAM-2 Guideline surface-to-air missile. Beginning in the mid-1960s, a total of 108 V-750 launchers were delivered to the Hungarian Air Force National Air Defense Command. Both the Yak-28R and the SAM-2 were once exhibits in a park near Debrecen before they were removed

and taken to the Aeroking KFT storage depot.

The majority of the aircraft in storage are MiG-15bis fighters from Soviet and Czech production. There are also three MiG-17PFs, two MiG-19PMs, a number of MiG-21F-13s and a single MiG-21U Mongol. The Frescos and Farmers were used in limited numbers by the Hungarian Air Force (fifteen MiG-17PF and twelve MiG-19PMs). Hungary was the first export customer of the Fishbed. The first MiG-21F-13 being delivered on 6 March 1960.

Most of the MiG fighters carry four digit tactical numbers. It is generally known that the MiG-15 and MiG-21F-13 carried three digit numbers and the MiG-17PF and MiG-19PM had two digit Red tactical numbers during their operational service. So the four digit numbers are believed to have been applied after the aircraft were struck off charge. It must be noted; however, that with the introduction of the MiG-21PF, MiG-21MF and MiG-21bis, the tactical number was changed to four digits. The reason for this was that the Hungarian's always repeat the

A MiG-17PF, Red 1975, at Vecses. The burned canopy indicates that this aircraft was used for fire fighting training duties. Only fifteen MiG-17PF were delivered to Hungary.

This badly damaged MiG-19PM Farmer, Red 1978, once served with the 31st Fighter Regiment based at Taszar, Hungary. A total of twelve Farmers were delivered to the Hungarian Air Force during March and April of 1960 to replace the MiG-17PF in the all weather interceptor role.

A line-up of some of the various MiG fighter held in storage at Vecses. The condition of the aircraft varies from very good, to badly damage (beyond economical repair). A total of forty-one aircraft are stored at Vecses.

last digits of the manufacturer number as the tactical number on the nose. With the arrival of a large numbers of Fishbeds it happened that the ending three digits were often the same which could result redundant tactical numbers, to prevent this, four digit tactical number were used.

The Aeroking KFT storage depot can be visited after getting advance permission. I had no trouble in obtain permission on either of my two visits to the depot in July and August of 1992.

The tail section of this MiG-21F-13 Fishbed C was damaged during transport to the storage yard. Additionally, part of the dorsal spine covering is also missing. The Fishbed C did not carry the national insignia on the fuselage side. It was carried on the fin and on the wing undersurfaces only.

A MiG-21F-13 fuselage lies on its side next to the fuselage of a MiG-15, with the wing of the collection's Yak-28R in the foreground. Parts of the Yak-28R were spread in a wide circle within the storage depot.

A badly damaged MiG-21F-13 fuselage on the ground in the storage depot. The entire canopy is missing, giving a good view of the armor-glass screen that was placed inside the canopy. This airframe will be a source of parts for the restoration of others within the collection.

(Left) The sole MiG-21U Mongol in the collection, Red 1320, is placed near the entrence to the Vecses storage depot. The Mongol has its original tactical number, one of the few aircraft in the collection with its original number. The aircraft has part of the air data sensor boom missing. Other than that, it is in very good condition.

A pair of overall Olive Green Mi-1 Hare helicopters are stored at Vecses. The helicopter on the left is actually a Polish built SM-1, while the canibalized fuselage on the right is an original Soviet built Mi-1. The rotor blades for both helicopters are stored elsewere on the depot.

MiG-21UMs which remained in Hungarian Air Force service received the pre-war national markings. These markings have replaced the cold war era Red star marking on all Hungarian aircraft. (Laszlo Javor)

This SA-2 Guideline (SAM-2) surface-to-air anti-aircraft guided missile was once displayed at a park in Debrecen. The missile and its launcher are now stored at Vecses. In front of the SAM is a pair of MiG-15wings in wooden storage containers. The aircraft in the foreground is a MiG-19PM all weather fighter. (Josef Simon)

The area behind the Mi-1 Hare helicopters is littered with MiG-21 nose sections, the tail of the Yak-28 and rotor blades for the Mi-1s. The uncovered aircraft framework is part of a Polish-built PZL-101 Gawron

Before coming to Vecses, the Yak-28 and SA-2 were displayed in a park at Debrecen. The Yak-28 was presented to the town by the Soviet reconnaissance unit that was based there.

The framework of a PZL-101 rests along side an An-2 Colt biplane transport. The PZL-101 was a Polish development of the Soviet Yak-12M

This An-2M Colt is complete and can be restored. The wings are elsewhere in the depot. This aircraft served in the military, then was later used as a crop sprayer, carrying the civil registration HA-MHJ. The dog house in the foreground is the home of the depots two guard dogs.

(Left) This An-2M fuselage carries the civil registragion HA-MHF on the fuselage in Black. This aircraft and one other will probably serve as sources of spare parts for the restoration of An-2 HA-MHJ.

The lack of the usual fabric skinning, gives a good view of the construction of the Polish PZL-101 (Yak-12M). Components for the entire aircraft are stored withing the yard, although they are scattered.

This badly damaged An-2 has all the canopy glass broken out ant numerous holes in the fuselage. It is unlikely that this aircraft could be restored, it will more than likely end up a source of parts for other restorations.

This MiG-15UTI Midget carried the tactical number Red 771 when it was in active service. The Midget has had all national markings and unit markings stripped from the airframe. The wing glove panel is missing.

(Right)The forward fuselage of a MiG-15UTI Midget, Red 1975, minus its wings, is parked on its belly at Vecses. The entire rear fuselage section has been removed, revealing the installation of the VK-1 turbojet engine. The Klimov VK-1 engine is damage and the rear combustion chamber is missing. The VK-1 was a copy of the British Nene engine. Another MiG-15UTI is directly behind it with the canopy missing.

This MiG-15UTI, Red 1975, has a thin White outline around the tactical number. The aircraft rests on its nose wheel and tail skin in the Aeroking storage depot. The wings, stabilators and the upper portion of the fin had been removed as have both ejection seats.

Some of the stored MiG-15bis fighters in the depot have sustained heavy damage before they were removed to the storage depot. This aircraft has had the plexiglass canopy broken and the R-800 radio was removed from the nose compartment. The engine in the foreground is a ASh-62IR radial engine used on the Li-2 transport.

(Left) This MiG-21F-13, Red 1981, has the canopy class smashed out, a section of the upper fuselage spine missing and the air data boom, normally carried under the nose center section, removed, Hungary was the world's first export customer of the MiG-21Fishbed, with he first aircraft being delivered on 6 March 1960.

A line-up of some of the MiG-15bis and MiG-17PF fighters in storage at Vecses. Some of the aircraft were reasembled after their arrival in the depot while a number were not. The two aircraft in the foreground are MiG-15s while the third aircraft in line is a MiG-17PF all-weather fighter.